T0271616

THE
Authentic
Ukrainian
Kitchen

YEVHEN KLOPOTENKO

THE Authentic Ukrainian Kitchen

RECIPES FROM A NATIVE CHEF

PHOTOGRAPHS BY DIMA BAHTA
AND VLADYSLAV NAHORNYI

ROBINSON

ROBINSON

First published in the United States in 2024 by
Voracious/Little, Brown and Company,
an imprint of Hachette Book Group

First published in Great Britain in 2024 by
Robinson

10 9 8 7 6 5 4 3 2 1

A CIP catalogue record for this book
is available from the British Library.

Photographs (recipes) by Dima Bahta
Photographs of Chef Klopotenko by Vladyslav
Nahornyi

Ukrainian team:
Executive producer: Oleksandra Fidkevych
Project editor: Oleksandra Povoroznyk
Food producer and food stylist: Oleksii
Tatianchenko
Cooks: Yevhen Klopotenko and Viacheslav
Shulhin

ISBN: 978-1-47214-854-4

Printed and bound in Italy by L.E.G.O. S.p.A

Papers used by Robinson are from well-
managed forests and other responsible
sources.

Robinson
An imprint of
Little, Brown Book Group
Carmelite House
50 Victoria Embankment
London EC4Y 0DZ

An Hachette UK Company

www.hachette.co.uk

www.littlebrown.co.uk

contents

Breakfast

62

Salads

86

Soup & Borsch

110

Main Dishes

130

Sweets
190

Drinks
240

To all fallen defenders and those who are fighting for the free future of Ukraine!

introduction

THE TRUE COOKING OF UKRAINE

Throughout most of its history, Ukrainian cuisine developed in the same way as other regional cuisines. It reflected the abundance of local produce, absorbed foreign influences during times of trade and war, and gradually separated into three distinct culinary styles: the refined food of the upper classes, the simple and nourishing meals prepared by workers, and the hearty dishes traditionally favoured by villagers.

Then the unforeseeable happened: In the twentieth century, Ukrainian territory was absorbed by the Soviet Union (some parts sooner, some later). The USSR wasn't just another imperialist force intent on colonizing Ukraine but a behemoth determined to eradicate the heritages of its ethnic minorities and create a new, faceless, hegemonized culture devoid of individuality and regional differences.

Eighty years of Soviet rule wiped out entire generations of Ukrainian artists, dissidents, and philosophers. It also changed the way the overwhelming majority of Ukrainians thought, dressed, and even ate. To come up with a new, ideologically correct food culture, the Soviets turned to French cuisine—or a bastardized version of it. Olivier salad, a czarist-era delicacy invented by Moscow-based chef Lucien Olivier, was adapted to make use of readily available ingredients such as cheap sausage, boiled potatoes, and canned peas. Regional varieties of bread were replaced by simple mass-produced wheat loaves cryptically named baton. The word *compote,* or *kompot,* now referred to a sugary beverage made from boiled fruit. It became a staple in every stolovaya, the government-run canteens catering to factory workers and university students.

Elements of regional cuisines (such as Ukrainian borsch and Georgian kharcho) were carefully incorporated into this carb-laden, heavily regulated diet, but with alterations: local spices and seasonal ingredients were out, as were flavours that were deemed too "exotic."

Meanwhile, authentic Ukrainian cuisine—the incredibly varied dishes once lovingly prepared by our ancestors—went into hiding. For almost a century, this cooking could be found only in the tucked-away villages, the recipes passed from one generation to another in secret. While other regional cuisines changed and absorbed foreign techniques, welcomed new ingredients, and took inspiration from one another, Ukrainian recipes remained unchanged and, for the most part, unknown. So unknown, in fact, that when the Soviet Union finally fell apart and Ukrainians were left with a bland, carb-heavy diet meant to quickly and cheaply feed as many people as possible, many believed that this was what Ukrainian food had *always* been like.

Undoing the damage done by the Soviet system isn't a simple process. For one thing, it means fighting ridiculous food-related regulations literally written into our laws. Here's just one example: Until early 2022, the cafeterias in Ukrainian schools, universities, and other government-run institutions were officially forbidden to use herbs and spices and instead relied on generous helpings of salt to give the dishes some semblance of flavour. These dishes were precisely what many people enjoyed. They reminded them of their childhood years, and nostalgia is a tough opponent to battle.

But we are bringing real Ukrainian cuisine out of hiding. Cooks here and across the world are realizing what a treasure trove of history and flavour there is! In 2022, UNESCO added borsch to its List of Intangible Cultural Heritage in Need of Urgent Safeguarding, and, for the first time in decades, many Ukrainians felt proud of their culinary heritage and curious to discover more of it.

Thankfully, many non-Ukrainians share this newfound interest. As our nation bravely resists the Russian invasion, people all over the world are discovering Ukrainian literature, cinema, history, music, and food. After all, if you want to learn about a culture, what better way than to try its dishes? Despite what the Soviets believed, food isn't just about sustenance. It can take you on an exhilarating trip through a nation's history, teach you about its people's preferences and dislikes and relationships with their neighbors, and, well, give you a taste of the region.

This book is about the real cooking of Ukraine, the food Ukrainians once prepared and ate at home and for celebrations, and the food we make in our modern lives today. This food reflects the lifestyles of people from the Donetsk region, Crimea, Bukovyna, Podillia, and across the entire territory of Ukraine. These dishes carry the identity of our region and bring people even closer together. When a family from Kyiv cooks the food of a family from Slobozhanshchyna, it is a display of respect and unity. And when Americans or Italians or citizens of any other country follow a Ukrainian recipe, what is it but the preservation of Ukraine's traditions and history?

You will find dishes both familiar and forgotten, from borsch in its many forms to varenyky, our dumplings stuffed with savoury or sweet fillings. We begin many meals with bread, and our love of dips and spreads is on display. You'll see fresh ideas for using common vegetables, interesting approaches to pickling and preservation, hearty stews and roasted dishes, more than a few excellent things to drink, and the delight of simple baked goods and desserts such as Kyiv candied fruit and Lviv cheesecake.

But who am I to tell you about the world of Ukrainian food? I was born into an ordinary Ukrainian family that had nothing to do with the culinary world. But my grandmother moved to the United Kingdom in 1991 and invited me to live with her, and that experience opened a new world of food for me. After I left Great Britain, I spent time in Italy and worked as a waiter in restaurants across Germany, the United States, and Ukraine. One day, as I was standing in the middle of a kitchen and watching chefs at work, it struck me that this was what I wanted to do. At first, it was all fun and games; with friends, I created the CookWars cooking competition, which grew into an evening show in one of the Kyiv restaurants. Next was *MasterChef Ukraine*. Winning this show gave me the means to implement much larger projects and enabled me to study at Le Cordon Bleu in Paris.

Along the way I began to ask myself: why do I know more about the regional cooking of, say, Italy than I do about the cooking of the place where I grew up? This was during a time when Russian aggression was showing us and the rest of the world that they did not believe Ukraine deserved to exist independently at all. I began to dig deeper to discover and promote the riches our cuisine has to offer.

Today, my main aspirations are to improve the food culture in Ukraine and strengthen the position of Ukrainian cuisine in the world. All my projects are aimed at this. I mentioned earlier the challenge of reversing Soviet-era mandates in our school cafeterias; in 2016, I launched a project called Cult Food to improve the nutrition in our schools. In 2020, more than five thousand schools were following my comprehensive meal manual, and in 2021, all kindergartens and schools in Ukraine switched to new food standards and norms.

I have published several cookbooks in Ukrainian, and my website, Klopotenko.com, is the most popular culinary website in the country. I also run two restaurants. The first, launched in 2019 in Kyiv, is 100 Rokiv Tomu Vpered (100 Years Back to the Future); it presents a modern form of Ukrainian cuisine. Its aims are to show what Ukrainian cuisine would look like if it weren't for the Soviet Union and to challenge the stereotype that our cuisine consists solely of borsch and varenyky. Later, in the midst of the full-scale Russian invasion in 2022, I launched Inshi Bistro in Lviv, which provides food to those who, for one reason or another, are unable to pay. Inshi has two menus, the main menu and menu number two. People can order free of charge from the latter. In 2023, we continued to introduce Ukrainians to local dishes and drinks and opened the restaurant Poltava in Kyiv and the bar Inshi in Lviv.

Here, in this book, I am sharing my experiences, enthusiasm, and knowledge with you. These recipes and stories are but tiny drops in the sea of knowledge about Ukrainian food, but I hope they will make you want to dive in and discover more about this culture that has so much to offer. Perhaps these recipes will even help you step into Ukrainians' shoes—if only for a minute—and understand us as an independent people with a unique culture all our own.

THE UKRAINIAN PANTRY

Ukrainian cuisine has developed as part of a larger European cuisine throughout its history, both influenced by and influencing the regional cuisines of our closest neighbors. The cooking techniques and recipes of many Ukrainian dishes are similar to those found in Hungarian, Polish, and even German cuisines. But still, there are many ingredients that we immediately associate with Ukrainian cooking, and they deserve a mention.

I'd also like to talk a little about the flavour profiles of Ukrainian dishes, and the best way to do this is by using borsch as an example. The iconic Ukrainian dish combines both sweetness from ripe beetroots and acidity from tomatoes, and you'll find this combo in most of the foods we love. However, you probably won't find a lot of salt or spicy heat in our cuisine, except maybe when it comes to fermented vegetables, savoury sheep's-milk cheese, and the cured meats popular in the mountainous Carpathian region. So if some of the recipes in this book are a little light on the salt or not spicy enough for you, keep in mind that this is what authentic Ukrainian food tastes like. But you can always adjust the seasoning.

Beetroots

My list of iconic Ukrainian ingredients begins with beetroots—a vegetable that's simply a must-have to make borsch. (My classic recipe is on page 118. As previously noted, the Ukrainian method of making borsch was added to UNESCO's List of Intangible Cultural Heritage in Need of Urgent Safeguarding on July 1, 2022.) And although beetroot-based dishes can be found in other cuisines around the globe, I'm convinced that Ukrainians are the biggest beetroot lovers in the world.

If you didn't think beetroots were versatile, just look at Beetroot Kvas (page 244), a traditional fermented drink that can be added to borsch, used for braising meat, or enjoyed as a refreshing summertime drink. As you can tell from all our beetroot-based salads and snacks, beetroots are an integral part of any Ukrainian person's diet. Beetroot-heavy dishes are prepared on holidays and as simple weekday dinners, and the humble root vegetable can be boiled, baked, fried, and even pickled to last through the winter. In this book you will find many dishes with this vegetable and I hope that at least a few of them become staples in your home.

Rye flour and bread

Thanks to the fertile black soil Ukraine has always been famous for, rye and other grains have always grown in abundance. Traditional Rye Bread (page 19) is made from rye flour—another staple in the Ukrainian pantry—and has historically been the loaf on which Ukrainians relied for sustenance. Festive breads, such as korovai (bread served at weddings) and celebratory paskas, were usually made using wheat flour. Bread was traditionally naturally leavened using sourdough starters, although later the use of yeast became widespread.

For centuries, bread was a sacred symbol of wealth and well-being. Throwing uneaten bread away or letting it go bad was akin to blasphemy, and if there were any crumbs left over after a meal, they were given to poultry or livestock. In the twentieth century, rye bread was supplanted by the Soviet wheat loaf, and although the habit of eating white bread is still strong, more and more Ukrainians are going back to eating rye bread.

Wheat and baked goods

Along with rye, wheat occupies an important place in Ukrainian cuisine. Wheat berries are the basis of Kutya (page 212), an iconic dish served on Christmas Eve. And wheat flour was traditionally used to prepare almost all festive baked goods—cakes, buns, paskas. Today, unmilled wheat berries are undeservedly forgotten as an ingredient and appear on the tables of Ukrainians only at Christmas. However, wheat flour is now used to make the majority of baked goods.

Buckwheat

Buckwheat is so popular in Ukraine that, according to Google, *how to cook buckwheat* was the most common food-related search in the country for the past several years. Curiously enough, buckwheat (or, as we call it, hrechka) wasn't always this widely used in Ukraine, and it's a bit of a mystery as to how it first arrived in the country. Some sources claim that it was brought to what is now the territory of modern Ukraine by Tatars in the tenth or eleventh century, and that's why certain Slavic languages refer to the crop as tatarka. But

PICTURED OPPOSITE:

● beetroots for kvas,
● rye flour for traditional rye bread,
● wheat berries in kutya,
● salo and garlic dip

archaeologists are fairly certain that buckwheat had been cultivated in Ukraine even earlier than that.

Whatever the case, buckwheat rose to prominence somewhere in the sixteenth or seventeenth century, and Ukraine became Europe's biggest producer of it. Back in those days, the grain was usually ground up into buckwheat flour that was used to make varenyky (savoury or sweet hand pies) and cooked into a lemishka (crispy flatbread).

Corn

Corn is quite popular in Ukraine. It is impossible to pinpoint exactly how it arrived here. According to some historical sources, when it first appeared in Ukraine in the eighteenth century, it came from Turkey through the Crimea; other sources say it came through Mouldova. Whatever the case, during corn season, corn is usually boiled whole, smeared with butter, sprinkled with salt, and immediately devoured. Banosh (page 153)—a traditional Hutsul dish that remains one of the most popular dishes in the Carpathian region—is made from corn grits. (Hutsuls are an East Slavic ethnic group originally from western Ukraine and Romania.)

Salo

It is hard to imagine Ukrainian cuisine without this ingredient. Salo, or pork fatback, is the white layer of fat found under the pig's skin. It is used everywhere in Ukrainian dishes—as a fat for frying potatoes and eggs, a base for savoury spreads, and even as a stand-alone snack. You can serve it on a slice of rye bread, along with a bowl of borsch, or with a selection of cold cuts. It is an essential ingredient in homemade sausage, and salo cracklings are added to porridge, boiled potatoes, and dumplings. One of the most popular snacks that you can buy in any Ukrainian supermarket is a thick paste made from salo and finely minced garlic.

Kovbasa

Making kovbasa—a general term for a variety of sausages—was a great way to extend the shelf life of meat. In traditional Ukrainian cuisine, sausages were made mainly from pork, using the thin intestines of a boar or pig as casing. They were stuffed with minced or chopped meat and garlic and other spices; sometimes, a little lard was added to make the taste richer. In the central regions of Ukraine, sausages were pan-fried or oven-baked (Homemade Kovbasa with Garlic, page 158). In the western regions, sausage was often smoked and cured. Meat products prepared in this way were called vudzheni (the term literally means "smoked").

PICTURED OPPOSITE:

salo

We should also mention Krovianka (page 161), a sausage stuffed with blood, buckwheat, and lard. This type of sausage is usually fried or baked, and the filling depends on the specific region. For example, in Polissia, grated potatoes and breadcrumbs were traditionally added to the mixture, while in the Poltava and Chernihiv regions, corn or millet porridge was often used instead of buckwheat.

Bryndza

We can't talk about Hutsul cuisine without mentioning cheese. After all, the people of the mountainous Carpathian region have traditionally been involved in sheepherding, and sheep's-milk cheese has always been a staple of their diet. Sadly, a lot of traditions have been forgotten, and finding authentic Hutsul cheese can be a challenge! Proper bryndza is crumbly and salty, and if it's kept in a cool place, it stays fresh for a long time. Over the past few centuries, cheese made from goat's and cow's milk has been produced all over the country, but the taste differs from bryndza made by Hutsuls. You can add bryndza to all kinds of porridges—it is an essential ingredient in banosh!—or crumble it over a garden salad or a potato casserole. If you cannot find genuine bryndza cheese, good-quality sheep's-milk feta is an acceptable substitute.

Syr (soft cheese)

It is impossible to know for certain where and when Ukrainians began making syr, a soft cheese made from fermented cow's milk. But there's no denying that it's one of our most popular dairy products and has historically been made in all parts of the country. Syr is similar to ricotta in terms of both its taste and how it is produced. However, unlike the creamy ricotta, syr has a slightly grainy texture and is a little firmer. This firmness is what makes it the perfect ingredient for Syrnyky (Soft Cheese Pancakes, page 70) and a great filling for varenyky or crêpes.

Today you can buy countless kinds of syr in any Ukrainian supermarket, but the best stuff comes from the farmers' market. It's usually made from whole milk, has a high fat content, and is always fresh. You can even make it at home; all you need to do is curdle fresh unpasteurized milk at room temperature (it takes several days, but it's a very hands-off process), heat the curdled milk mixture to separate the whey, then filter the whey through muslin until the curds are relatively dry.

Of course, you can always replace syr with soft cheese, and that's what we call for in most of the recipes here.

Other fermented-milk products

Milk and cheese aren't the only dairy products Ukrainian cuisine is known for. Fermented-milk products such as soured cream are also traditionally popular.

PICTURED OPPOSITE:
- krovianka,
- banosh with bryndza,
- syr,
- pickled cucumbers

The Authentic Ukrainian Kitchen

You can find the recipe for soured cream in multiple cookbooks; it is made simply by curdling cream. Soured cream is added to pancakes and baked goods, served with soft cheese pancakes, and used when making desserts.

Kysliak (a Ukrainian type of buttermilk) is made simply by fermenting fresh milk; it's a refreshing drink. And if you're lucky enough to travel through the Carpathian Mountains, be sure to try the tangy drink guslianka. It is traditionally made using cow's milk that is boiled, cooled slightly, then transferred to a ceramic bowl containing a starter culture (usually leftover guslianka made the previous day) or soured cream. The milk is left to ferment for a day, sometimes after adding a little egg white.

Another popular drink made using fermented milk is ryazhanka. What sets it apart from the other similar dairy products is that the fermented milk is baked until it has a light golden colour and a subtle nutty flavour. Ryazhanka was traditionally made in wood-burning ovens.

Pickled vegetables

Meat was smoked and cured to keep it fresh during the cold winter months, and vegetables were traditionally pickled for the same reason. Cabbage, cucumbers, tomatoes, apples, and even watermelons were pickled in a brine in large wooden barrels that were stored in the cellar. These fermented vegetables were served as an appetizer to any meal and often used to prepare soups (for example, Kapusnyak, pickled cabbage soup, page 117, and soup with Pickled Cucumbers, page 56).

Horseradish

This peppery, pungent vegetable is a medicinal plant that improves digestion. It is also an essential ingredient in traditional Ukrainian cuisine and was once used as a talisman against evil forces. Grated horseradish and beetroots are used to make the spicy condiment Tsvikli (page 98), which is served along with meat or aspic (Kholodets, page 45). In some family recipes that have survived to this day, horseradish was added to meat while it was roasting in the oven. Horseradish is also used to make Khrinovuha (page 259), a strong infused vodka that is served in many Ukrainian restaurants.

Note: The food-preservation methods in this book are ones traditionally used by Ukrainians in their home kitchens. Pickling and canning are age-old traditions around the world, and the occasional exploding jar of fermented cucumbers or tomatoes is just accepted as part of home cooking. However, you may prefer a less casual approach to sterilizing jars of fermented produce that will be stored at room temperature. In that case, please keep pickles in the refrigerator instead and use them within a few weeks.

Alternatively, you can follow sterilization procedures for hot-water-bath canning as recommended by the U.S. National Center for Home Food Preservation: "All jams, jellies, and pickled products processed less than 10 minutes should be filled into sterile empty jars. To sterilize empty jars, put them right side up on the rack in a boiling-water canner. Fill the canner and jars with hot (not boiling) water to 1 inch above the tops of the jars. Boil 10 minutes at altitudes of less than 1,000 ft. At higher elevations, boil 1 additional minute for each additional 1,000 ft. elevation. Remove and drain hot sterilized jars one at a time. Save the hot water for processing filled jars. Fill jars with food, add lids, and tighten screw bands." For more information, visit https://nchfp .uga.edu.

Sunflower oil

Throughout 2021 and 2022 Ukraine was the largest producer of sunflowers in the world. Even today, in the midst of a brutal full-scale invasion, Ukraine remains one of the largest producers of this crop. But sunflowers aren't just a source of seeds and oil; they're also a symbol of the sun's energy and of health. You'll find sunflowers drawn on the walls of old Ukrainian houses and on various items from the Cossack era.

Today Ukrainians use refined sunflower oil for frying, as it has a neutral taste and a high smoking point, but salads are usually dressed with the fragrant unrefined oil. If you can hunt that down, please do so, as it will add a wonderful depth to your salads.

Herbs and spices

Dill and parsley are the most widely used herbs in Ukrainian cuisine. Ukrainians grow these herbs in their gardens even today; after all, who wouldn't want to have fresh, fragrant greens on the table? If dill isn't harvested in time, its shoots start to resemble umbrellas, but even these woody parts of the plant are put to good use—they are added to the brine when canning cucumbers and tomatoes.

Dried dill and parsley are components of merudiya, a Bessarabian spice blend known since ancient times; it also contains dried fenugreek and ginger mint.

Modern Ukrainians use spices from all over the world: black pepper and allspice, bay leaves, turmeric, and ginger. That is why you'll come across them in the recipes of this book.

Of course, this is far from a complete list of the ingredients used in Ukrainian cuisine. In fact, you could probably tell a separate story (or even write a separate book!) about dozens of widely used Ukrainian foods. But I am sure that after preparing only a few recipes with these few ingredients, you'll get a taste of Ukraine.

Bread
& Dips

quick palyanytsya bread

| makes one 7-inch (18-centimetre) round loaf | start to finish: 1 hour 10 minutes |

Швидкий рецепт паляниці

The first written recipes for palyanytsya, a round wheat loaf traditionally cooked in a hearth, date back to the nineteenth century, and most of them call for a yeasted dough made with a sourdough starter. So that the bread will rise better and to give it a softer texture, bakers make a small semicircular incision on top of the loaf before placing it in the oven. But in the early months of the full-scale Russian invasion in 2022, grocery stores all over the country were half empty, and even simple ingredients such as yeast were hard to come by, so I came up with a simplified version of this historical recipe that can easily be made at home using just a few pantry staples.

This version calls for bicarbonate of soda instead of yeast, and although it isn't as fluffy as the classic, it's still delicious. It's slightly chewy and has a crispy golden crust, perfect for sandwiches or to go alongside a steaming bowl of soup. But my favourite way to eat palyanytsya is to spread butter over a still-warm slice and sprinkle a little salt on top.

Curiously, the word *palyanytsya* became a kind of code that helped differentiate between Ukrainian and Russian soldiers during the early weeks of the war. While Russian-speaking Ukrainians know this word and have no trouble pronouncing it, native Russians often confuse it with *polunitsa*, which means "strawberry," or mispronounce it, because the Ukrainian and Russian languages are similar but different in key ways. For many Ukrainian soldiers, the humble palyanytsya became a symbol of belonging and clarity at a heartbreaking and confusing time.

4 cups (540 grams) plain flour, plus more for dusting
1 teaspoon bicarbonate of soda
1 teaspoon coarse salt
1⅔ cups (425 millilitres) plain kefir (or buttermilk or natural yogurt)
Vegetable oil, if kneading by hand

1. Preheat the oven to 200°C/400°F/Gas 6. Line a baking sheet with baking paper or a silicone baking mat.

2. In the bowl of a stand mixer, stir together the flour, bicarbonate of soda, and salt. Using a spatula, fold in the kefir (or buttermilk or yogurt). Mix everything together using the dough-hook attachment until a uniform and sticky dough forms, but take care to avoid overworking the dough. (This can also be done by hand: start by mixing the dough with a wooden spoon, then lightly grease your hands with vegetable oil and knead it out.)

3. Transfer the dough to a lightly floured work surface. Using lightly floured hands, knead it until it becomes smooth and just a little tacky

recipe continues

to the touch, about 5 minutes. If the dough is too sticky, sprinkle a little flour over it as you go. Keep adding the flour until the dough is comfortable to work with.

4. Form the dough into a roughly rectangular shape, flattening it lightly with your palms. Then fold the upper corners of the dough rectangle down, as if making an envelope. Fold the lower corners up so that they overlap. Flip the dough over so the seams are now on your kitchen surface. Using both hands, lightly cup the dough and tuck the edges underneath, shaping it into a ball. Rotate the dough as you go.

5. Transfer the dough ball, seam-side down, to the prepared baking sheet, cover it with a clean and dry kitchen towel, and let it rest for about 15 minutes to let the gluten relax a bit. Then make an incision on the surface of the dough ball to let the steam escape while baking. Bake the palyanytsya in the preheated oven for 40 to 45 minutes or until it is golden brown and baked through.

traditional
rye bread

makes	start to finish:
1 medium loaf	*2 hours*
	20 minutes

pictured on pages 20–21

Житній хліб

Rye bread holds a special place in traditional Ukrainian cuisine. Bread made from rye flour first gained popularity because it was cheaper than loaves made of wheat. Mention of this bread can be found in historical chronicles dating back to the Kyivan Rus, Ukraine's historic antecedent, about a thousand years ago. In ancient times, rye bread was made with a sourdough starter—a fermented portion of dough—and the recipe was a closely guarded secret kept by bread-making masters. Today, commercially available dried yeast is more commonly used for baking. Rye bread is darker in colour than wheat-flour palyanytsya and has a more robust flavour. Just smear a slice of fresh rye bread with ground salo or butter, and you will understand why Ukrainians are so fond of it!

1 cup (250 millilitres) warm water
1 tablespoon easy-bake/fast-action yeast
1 teaspoon granulated sugar
1½ cups (200 grams) strong bread flour
1 cup plus 2 tablespoons (100 grams) rye flour
2 tablespoons sunflower oil (or other neutral oil), plus more if kneading by hand
½ teaspoon coarse salt

1. To make a starter for the dough, combine the warm water, yeast, and sugar in a small bowl. Cover with a kitchen towel and let rest in a warm place until the mixture becomes foamy, about 5 minutes.

2. In the bowl of a stand mixer (or just a large bowl, if doing this by hand), combine both flours, the oil, and the yeast mixture. Using a dough-hook attachment, mix everything together until a sticky dough forms. If doing this by hand, start by mixing the dough with a wooden spoon until it starts coming together, then lightly grease your hands with a little oil and knead the dough for a few minutes or until it becomes elastic and sticky.

3. Transfer the dough to a greased medium bowl, cover with plastic wrap or a kitchen towel, and let rest in a warm, draft-free place for about 50 minutes or until it doubles in size.

4. Preheat the oven to 200°C/400°F/Gas 6 and line a baking sheet with baking paper or a silicone baking mat. Dust it with flour. Set aside.

5. Gently press down on the risen dough with your hands so some of the air is released. Lightly dust your kitchen surface with flour and transfer the dough onto it. Lightly knead the dough again until it becomes smooth and isn't as puffy anymore. Form the dough into a roughly rectangular shape, flattening it lightly with your palms. Then fold the upper corners of the dough rectangle down, as if making an envelope. Fold the lower corners up, so that they overlap. Flip the dough over so the seams are now on your kitchen surface. Using both hands, lightly cup the dough and tuck the edges underneath, shaping it into a ball. Transfer the ball onto the lined baking sheet, cover it with a slightly moist kitchen towel, and let rest for 30 more minutes.

6. Remove the kitchen towel and bake for 35 to 40 minutes.

garlic pampushky

traditional garlic bread rolls   *Пампушки з часником*

makes
12 rolls

start to finish:
2 hours

Pampushky—soft, round little bread rolls—are a lovely addition to any meal. They can be savoury and served alongside dips or with a spicy garlic-and-oil mixture, or they can be sweet and served as a stand-alone dessert topped with icing sugar or jam. Although all varieties of pampushky are popular, savoury bread rolls with garlic are particularly beloved as a perfect accompaniment to a hot bowl of thick, vibrantly coloured borsch.

These bread rolls are simple, but they'll elevate your dinner to new heights. You can serve these pampushky as an appetizer, or dip pieces of the soft, pillowy rolls right into the borsch as you eat. Just make sure to be generous with the garlicky dipping sauce, especially if you're making this dish during the colder months. According to Ukrainian folklore, eating hearty, garlic-heavy dishes is the secret to keeping yourself warm during the notoriously cold Eastern European winters, and if you eat enough garlic, you can even, it is said, stave off illness.

1. Combine the flour, yeast, sugar, and salt in a medium bowl and mix well. Then add the warm milk and the softened butter (or vegetable oil).

2. Mix everything until thoroughly combined and an elastic dough forms. Keep kneading it with your hands or a dough hook until the dough is no longer sticky. Shape the dough into a ball, place it in an oiled bowl, cover with a towel or plastic wrap, and let rest in a warm place for 40 to 45 minutes. It should roughly double in size.

3. Preheat the oven to 180°C/350°F/Gas 4. After the dough has rested, knead it a little more and divide it into 12 round balls. Thoroughly brush an 8-inch (20-centimetre) square baking dish with butter or oil, transfer the dough balls into the dish, placing them about ¼ inch (5 millimetres) apart, and let them rest for 30 more minutes. They will rise a little more while they rest.

4. Place the baking dish in the preheated oven and bake for 25 to 30 minutes or until the rolls are fluffy and golden brown.

5. While the pampushky are baking, make the topping: peel and finely mince the garlic cloves. Wash the dill sprigs, pat them dry, and mince finely. Combine the minced garlic and dill in a small bowl with the sunflower oil and vinegar. Add salt and pepper to taste and mix well.

6. When the rolls are out of the oven and still hot, generously glaze them with the garlic-oil mixture.

for the dough

3¼ cups (425 grams) strong bread flour

1 tablespoon easy-bake/fast-action yeast

1 tablespoon granulated sugar

½ teaspoon coarse salt

1 cup plus 1 tablespoon (260 millilitres) warm whole milk

3½ ounces (100 grams) unsalted butter, softened, or 3 tablespoons vegetable oil (plus extra to coat the baking dish)

for the garlic-oil topping

2 to 3 garlic cloves, to taste

5 sprigs fresh dill

2 tablespoons sunflower oil (or other neutral oil)

1 tablespoon white wine vinegar

Coarse salt and freshly ground black pepper to taste

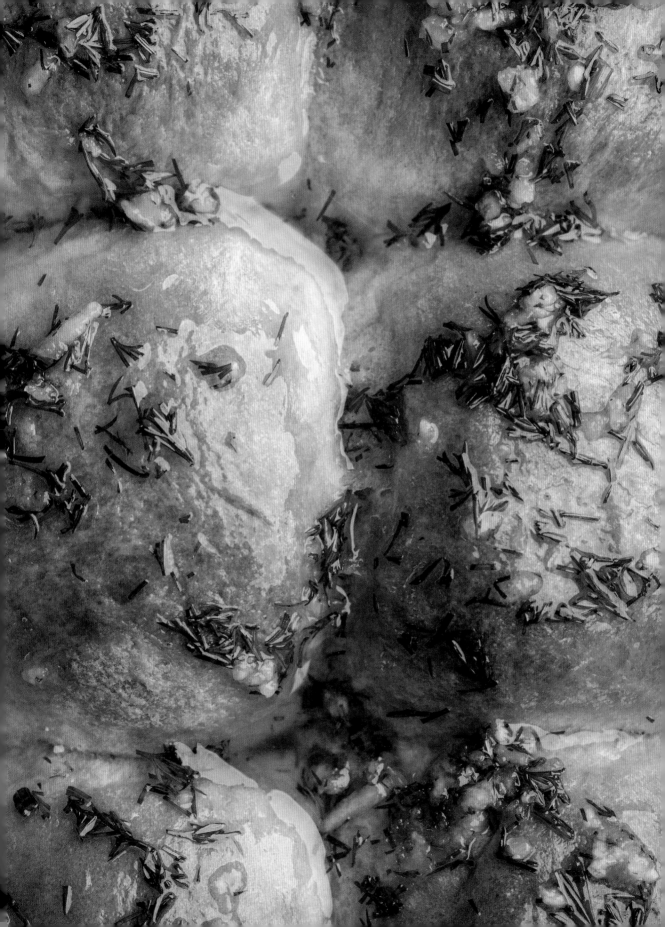

vorschmack

chopped herring spread *Форшмак*

This herring spread was perfected by Odesa's vibrant Jewish community. Traditionally, vorschmack is made with only herring, onion, and hard-boiled eggs, but most Odesa cooks cannot imagine this appetizer without the addition of a crisp, slightly tart apple. I know; apples, eggs, and herring might sound like an odd combination, but this humble dish is much more than the sum of its parts—it's a creamy sweet-and-savoury treat with a hint of tartness. Vorschmack can be served as an appetizer or a snack (in fact, the German word *vorschmack* translates to "a meal before a meal"). Just spread it on some good rye bread or some whole-grain crackers or serve it along with boiled potatoes.

To make this spread authentic, you need Danube-caught herring preserved with salt in large wooden barrels. But if you can't find that, use any other kind of salted herring in brine. To ensure that the spread comes out the way it should, do not use herring preserved in oil, and find some tart, crisp apples. If you're sensitive to salt, the herring can be soaked for an hour or two in milk and then dried with kitchen paper, which will make the flavour a little less intense.

1. Using a box grater, grate the apple and set it aside. Grate the onion and set it aside. Peel the hard-boiled eggs.

2. Quarter the eggs and cut the salted herring fillets into pieces small enough to go through a meat grinder. (If you don't have a meat grinder, you can use a food processor.)

3. Put the herring pieces and the quartered eggs through the meat grinder or blend them in a food processor. If using a food processor, don't blend the mixture for too long; it should remain a little chunky.

4. In a small bowl, combine the grated apple, grated onion, olive oil, and herring-and-egg mixture. It should end up slightly chunky but well combined.

5. Serve cold along with lightly toasted rye bread. Vorschmack can be made ahead; it will stay fresh for two to three days if kept in a lidded jar in the refrigerator.

1 Granny Smith apple, peeled and cored
½ medium onion, peeled
2 large eggs, hard-boiled
10 ounces (280 grams) salted herring fillets
2 tablespoons extra-virgin olive oil
Traditional Rye Bread (page 19), for serving

salo and garlic dip

Сало перетерте з часником

Salo is the Ukrainian word for salt-cured pork fatback; it's similar to Italian lardo and American fatback or bacon but with little or no lean meat. For everyone who wants to feel a little Ukrainian, ground-up salo with garlic is a must. This snack is so popular that it is sold in almost every Ukrainian supermarket. To get the full experience, spread it on a slice of toasted rye bread and serve along with a steaming bowl of hot borsch.

1. Cut the salo into cubes or strips thin enough to fit into a meat grinder.

2. Alternating between the cubes of salo and the garlic cloves, put all the ingredients through the meat grinder. You will end up with a pâté-like mixture that can be used as a dip or spread on crusty rye bread as an appetizer. If you don't have a meat grinder, you can blend everything in a food processor (just make sure not to overblend!) or simply chop everything up finely with a sharp kitchen knife and mix well to combine. The dip can be stored in a lidded jar in the refrigerator for three to five days.

**makes about
1 pound
(450 grams)**

start to finish:
10 minutes

1 pound (450 grams) salo
Cloves from ½ to 1 garlic bulb, to taste, peeled and crushed

––––––
Optional: If desired, trim the skin off the pork fatback.

roasted garlic and herb butter

Масло із запеченим часником

Bread and butter is probably the most popular appetizer in the whole world. Each country has its own variations of this simple but tasty dish. Some cuisines add traditional herbs, fish, or even meat to the butter to give it a twist. If you want to fully experience the Ukrainian taste, add a hint of garlic to your butter—not fresh garlic, because it is too sharp and pungent, but roasted, with nutty notes and a pleasant smoky aroma. Generously spread it on a freshly toasted slice of bread and wait for it to melt and permeate the crumb. It will be incredibly delicious!

Whole roasted garlic bulb,
   unpeeled
1 teaspoon sunflower oil (or other
   neutral oil)
7½ ounces (210 grams) unsalted
   butter, brought to room
   temperature
A few sprigs dill
Freshly ground black pepper to
   taste

1. Preheat the oven to 180°C/350°F/Gas 4.

2. Cut off about a quarter of the garlic top so the cloves are slightly exposed. Place the garlic bulb in a rectangular piece of aluminum foil and drizzle a little oil over the exposed garlic cloves. Wrap the garlic tightly in the aluminum foil and place on a baking tray or in an oven-safe dish.

3. Bake the garlic bulb in the preheated oven for about 30 minutes or until fragrant and soft. Remove from the oven and let cool completely.

4. Meanwhile, transfer the softened butter to a small mixing dish. Finely mince the dill (only the leaves; discard the stems) and add it to the butter.

5. Once the garlic is cool enough to handle, squeeze out the cloves (they should be soft enough to be squeezed out by hand) and add them to the butter. Add a few pinches of freshly ground black pepper. Mash everything with a fork until well combined.

6. Lay a piece of baking paper on your kitchen surface and turn the butter-and-herb mixture out onto it. Roll the butter into a log, wrap the baking paper around it, and twist the ends to close. Chill in the refrigerator until the butter solidifies completely. In an airtight container, it will keep in the refrigerator for about two weeks.

baked aubergine and pepper dip

serves 4 | start to finish: *40 minutes*

Баклажанна ікра з солодким перцем

Aubergine spread is one of the most popular vegetable-based appetizers in Ukrainian cuisine. We even call it "aubergine caviar," although it has nothing to do with real caviar; perhaps this is a tribute to the dish's exquisite taste. You can make a batch of this amazing spread and serve it immediately or jar it and preserve some for the winter. You'll get the best flavour by charring the aubergines on a charcoal grill instead of baking them in the oven, of course—the aroma of smoke goes very well with this dish. But even oven-baked aubergines make a wonderful spread.

2 small (or 1 large) red peppers
1 medium tomato
1 medium aubergine
3 garlic cloves, peeled
2 tablespoons sunflower oil (or other neutral oil)
½ teaspoon chilli powder
¼ ounce (10 grams) unsalted butter
Coarse salt to taste

1. Preheat the oven to 190°C/375°F/Gas 5. Line a baking sheet with baking paper and set aside.

2. Place the peppers, the tomato, the aubergine, and the peeled garlic cloves on the lined baking sheet and brush them with a little sunflower oil. Bake in the preheated oven for about 15 minutes or until the vegetables are fragrant, lightly charred, and can be pierced easily with a fork. Remove them from the oven, set aside, and let cool completely.

3. Once the vegetables are cool enough to handle comfortably, peel the aubergine using a sharp paring knife. The skin on the peppers and the tomato should be loose enough that you'll be able to peel it off using just your hands.

4. Transfer the peeled vegetables to your food processor or blender. Add the garlic cloves, the ground chilli, the butter, and a pinch of salt. Blend until smooth, drizzling in a little oil from time to time to help emulsify, and adjust seasoning if needed. Drizzle with a little more sunflower oil before serving.

easy mushroom dip

serves 6 | start to finish: *30 minutes*

Грибна ікра

Among the most popular dishes in Ukraine is mushroom caviar. Of course, like the previous aubergine-caviar recipe, this is not real caviar. It is simply a glorious dip made from finely chopped wild mushrooms. Wild mushrooms, which have been part of Ukrainian cuisine for a very long time, are found in Ukrainian forests, so this mushroom dip has historically been associated with the cuisine of the Carpathian Mountains and the Polissia and Poltava regions. In this recipe, I tried to re-create the taste using spices, cognac, and easy-to-find button mushrooms instead of wild ones. It's wonderful.

1 pound (450 grams) button mushrooms
1 ounce (30 grams) unsalted butter
2 to 3 pinches of ground coriander, to taste
2 garlic cloves, peeled
Coarse salt and freshly ground black pepper
2 tablespoons (30 millilitres) cognac or brandy
1 sprig parsley, chopped

1. Lightly wipe down the mushrooms with moist kitchen paper and discard the stem bottoms if they are too dirty to clean off without washing. Roughly chop the mushrooms and set aside.

2. Heat the butter in a medium frying pan over medium heat. Add the mushrooms in batches and sauté them until golden and fragrant. Do not overcrowd the pan or the mushrooms will release too much water and become soggy.

3. When frying the last batch, add the coriander, garlic cloves, and salt and pepper to taste. Add the cognac and keep sautéing everything until the mushrooms are golden brown and the liquid has evaporated. This will take several minutes. Once the mushrooms are nice and brown, take the pan off the heat, set aside, and let cool.

4. Using a blender or a food processor, blitz the mushrooms and garlic cloves until smooth. Adjust the seasoning to taste and let the dip cool completely in the fridge. Garnish with fresh parsley immediately before serving.

Appetizers

pyrizhky

stuffed with minced meat or split peas

Пиріжки з різними начинками

makes about
18 pies

start to finish:
*2 hours
50 minutes*

pictured on pages 40–41

Pyrizhky—little pies stuffed with all kinds of delicious fillings—are mentioned in Ivan Kotliarevskyy's humorous retelling of the *Aeneid*, considered one of the first works written in modern Ukrainian. According to the ever-ironic Kotliarevskyy, these little pockets of golden dough are the surest way to capture a woman's heart. I usually agree with Kotliarevskyy on pretty much everything, but this time I'd like to correct the legendary writer—pyrizhky are the surest way to capture *anyone's* heart.

If you want to know how popular pyrizhky are in Ukraine, stroll through any Ukrainian city and take a look at all the pyrizhvoki—cozy little cafés that serve nothing but these little pies. For this book, I couldn't choose only one type of filling, so I share the recipes for two incredibly popular types of pies, one stuffed with minced meat and one stuffed with split peas and onions. Try them both and make up your own mind which is better!

for the dough

- ⅓ cup plus 1 tablespoon (90 millilitres) warm water
- ½ cup plus 2 tablespoons (150 millilitres) warm whole milk
- 1 ounce (30 grams) fresh yeast
- 1 teaspoon granulated sugar
- 4 cups (540 grams) strong bread flour, plus 2 tablespoons (18 grams) for the starter
- 1 teaspoon coarse salt
- 3 tablespoons sunflower oil (or other neutral oil)
- 1 large egg
- 1 large egg yolk

Note: Instead of fresh yeast, you can use 2¼ teaspoons/ 7 grams easy-bake/fast-action yeast.

1. Make the dough starter: in a small bowl, combine the warm water and the milk. Make sure the liquid is warm but no hotter than 40°C/104°F. Crumble the fresh yeast into the bowl. Stir in the sugar and the 2 tablespoons flour. Cover the mixture with a clean kitchen towel and let rest in a warm, draft-free place for about 20 minutes or until it becomes frothy.

2. Make the dough: in a large bowl (or the bowl of a stand mixer), combine the 4 cups (540 grams) flour, the salt, the starter, the sunflower oil, and the whole egg. Using a wooden spoon or a dough-hook attachment, mix everything to combine until it becomes a cohesive, sticky dough. Form the dough into a ball, transfer it to a lightly oiled bowl, cover with a clean kitchen towel, and let rest in a warm, draft-free place for about 40 minutes or until doubled in size.

3. Meanwhile, make the two different fillings (or, if you prefer, two portions of the same filling).

    a. **To make the meat filling,** bring a large saucepan of water to a boil over medium-high heat and add the pork shoulder, bay leaf, and allspice. Reduce the heat and simmer the meat for about 1½ hours or until the internal temperature reaches 65°C/145°F. Heat some sunflower oil in a small pan over medium heat, add the diced onion, and sauté until golden and fragrant. Drain the water from the pork, let the meat cool completely, then cut it into small chunks and put it through a meat grinder. In a medium bowl, combine the ground pork and the sautéed onions, add salt and pepper to taste, and mix until thoroughly combined.

    b. **To make the pea filling,** bring a medium saucepan of water to a boil and add the presoaked and drained peas. Reduce heat, cover, and simmer until the peas are tender but not mushy. Drain and let cool completely. Meanwhile, heat the sunflower oil in a small pan over medium heat, add the diced onion, and sauté until golden and fragrant. Mash the cooked peas with a fork, then fold in the sautéed onions. Add salt and pepper to taste.

4. Preheat the oven to 180°C/350°F/Gas 4. Line a baking sheet with baking paper. Lightly dust a kitchen surface with a little flour and turn the dough onto it. Knead it until smooth and just a little tacky. Roll the dough into a ball and divide it into about 18 equal pieces (if you want the pies smaller, make more than 18; if you want them larger, make fewer). Roll the pieces of dough into flat circles, and, working with one piece at a time, place about a tablespoon of filling into the centre of each. Pinch the edges of the dough circle together and carefully shape each pie as desired; I make the meat-filled pies into boat-like shapes and keep the pea-filled ones round and puffy.

5. Place the pies, seam-side down, on the parchment-lined baking sheet. Beat the egg yolk in a cup or small bowl and, using a silicone brush, carefully brush it on the pies. Bake the pies in the preheated oven for 20 to 25 minutes or until golden and slightly browned and crispy around the edges.

for the meat filling

1 pound (450 grams) boneless pork shoulder
1 bay leaf
1 allspice berry
2 tablespoons sunflower oil (or other neutral oil)
1 large onion, peeled and finely diced
Coarse salt and freshly ground black pepper to taste

for the pea filling

10½ ounces (300 grams) dried split peas, soaked overnight in a bowl of cold water
2 tablespoons sunflower oil (or other neutral oil)
1 large onion, peeled and finely diced
Coarse salt and freshly ground black pepper to taste

kyivska perepichka

sausage in deep-fried pastry   *Київська перепічка*

makes 9 or 10
sausage rolls

start to finish:
*1 hour
30 minutes*

If I had to choose one culinary symbol associated with the city of
Kyiv, I'd select the legendary Kyivska perepichka—a juicy sausage
or hot dog nestled inside deep-fried pastry. There's only one place in
the world where you can get the *real,* authentic perepichka: a tiny
shop in the middle of a busy street in downtown Kyiv, a shop that is
always surrounded by a crowd of hungry tourists and locals. The recipe
remains a well-guarded secret, but after endless attempts and some
experimenting, I think I've finally cracked it.

1. Make the dough: in a medium bowl, combine the warm milk, yeast, and
   sugar. Whisk until well combined, then stir in the flour. Mix everything
   with a wooden spoon (or a stand mixer equipped with a dough-hook
   attachment) until a cohesive, slightly runny dough forms. Transfer it to
   a lightly oiled bowl, cover with a kitchen towel, and let rest in a warm,
   draft-free place for 40 to 45 minutes or until doubled in size.

2. Turn the dough out onto a lightly floured kitchen surface, knead
   thoroughly (we advise greasing your hands first), and shape into a ball.
   Divide into 9 or 10 equal parts. Carefully insert a hot dog or sausage
   into each ball of dough, shaping the dough around it with your fingers.
   The dough should fully enclose the sausage, and all the edges should be
   sealed tightly; if they're not, the dough might split during the deep-
   frying process.

3. In a medium, heavy-based pot, heat 2 to 3 inches (5 to 8 centimetres)
   of oil to 190°C/375°F. Carefully lower one or two of the dough-encased
   sausages into the oil, making sure not to overcrowd the saucepan. Cook
   on one side for 2 to 3 minutes or until golden, then cook on the other side
   for 1 minute or less until golden. Drain the fried pastries on a wire rack
   set over a large tray or on a plate lined with kitchen paper.

1¾ cups (450 millilitres) warm
  whole milk
1 packet (about 2¼ teaspoons/
  7 grams) easy-bake/fast-action
  yeast
1 tablespoon granulated sugar
5¼ cups (680 grams) strong bread
  flour, plus about ½ cup
  (60 grams) for dusting
1 large egg
Pinch of coarse salt
9 or 10 precooked hot dogs or
  sausages
About 1 litre oil for
  deep-frying

kholodets

aspic   Холодець

On Christmas and New Year's Eve, many Ukrainian homes are
filled with the aroma of boiled meat and various spices because the
kholodets (aspic made from a rich broth) is being cooked for the
festive dinner. Cooking kholodets is somewhat similar to making bone
broth, both of which require long simmering. Yes, you do need a lot of
time to make a batch, but nothing can beat its distinctive taste.

Ukrainians often cook kholodets using the recipes passed down
to them by their grandmothers, so we pay special attention to its
preparation. The dish dates back to medieval times; it was a favourite
of both the Ukrainian nobility and ordinary Ukrainians. In some
regions of Ukraine, this dish is known as dragli; in others, it is referred
to as studynets. It also has regional variations: cooks in the Poltava
region use a lot of pork and beef and add fresh vegetables, while in the
Chernihiv region, kholodets includes a generous amount of greens and
seasonings, making it very aromatic.

I cook kholodets with a cockerel and the pig's foot because, in
my opinion, it has a richer taste and sets better than one made with
poultry alone. It tastes best with hot mustard or grated horseradish.

1 pig's foot
1 chicken, giblets removed
2 to 3 garlic cloves, crushed
1 large carrot, peeled and roughly
   chopped
1 large onion, peeled and roughly
   chopped
12 cups (3 litres) water, plus extra
   to soak
3 or 4 allspice berries
2 or 3 bay leaves
Coarse salt and freshly ground
   black pepper

1. Thoroughly scrub the pig's foot and soak it in cold water for 2 hours.
   Cut the chicken into several large pieces (to help it fit into the
   saucepan). Transfer it to a large bowl, cover with cold water, and let
   soak also for 2 hours or slightly less.

2. Drain the meat and the pig's foot and transfer them to a large saucepan.
   Cover with fresh cold water, bring to a rapid boil, reduce the heat, and
   simmer for a few minutes. Take the saucepan off the heat, drain the
   water, and thoroughly wash the meat and the pig's foot under cold
   running water.

3. Return the meat and the pig's foot to the saucepan, cover with 12 cups
   (3 litres) cold water, and bring to a boil once again. Add the crushed
   garlic cloves, carrot, onion, allspice berries, and bay leaves. Reduce the
   heat and cook at a gentle simmer for 4 to 5 hours, adding more water if
   necessary and skimming off the foam.

4. After 4 to 5 hours, remove the saucepan from the heat. Season the
   broth to taste with salt and black pepper. Discard the pig's foot.
   Remove the chicken pieces from the saucepan and take the meat off
   the bones. Transfer the meat to a large, sealable container and, using 2
   forks, grate it into tiny pieces.

5. Strain the broth into a large bowl through a muslin-lined sieve, then
   repeat the process. Make sure the broth is as clear as possible.

6. Pour the broth into the container with the chicken meat. Place it in the
   fridge for at least 4 hours or overnight to set. When it's done, it should
   be firm and jiggly. Serve along with horseradish sauce.

chibereky

deep-fried Crimean Tatar turnovers   *Чібереки*

Deep-frying isn't really a typical method in Ukrainian cuisine, but there are a few iconic street-food dishes that just can't be made any other way. One of them is chiberek, an extremely popular Crimean Tatar meat pie.

If you read about this dish online, you'll probably see it referred to as cheburek. But cheburek is a more Slavic-sounding term that replaced the original Qirim word in the late 1930s, when the Soviet Union was trying especially hard to assimilate Crimeans and erase the culture and heritage of the peninsula's indigenous people. The Latin alphabet, used for writing in Qirim, was replaced by Cyrillic, and many words and sounds were lost. Fortunately, today more and more people are learning about Crimean culture and rediscovering what Qirim words originally sounded like. Ukrainian restaurants are starting to replace the adapted Soviet-era names of Crimean dishes with the proper terms.

But let's get back to the dish itself. Just imagine: tender ground meat encased in thin, crispy, golden-brown dough…impossible to resist! And the best thing about chibereky is that, as intimidating as they appear, they're straightforward to make at home. The main thing is to get the dough right (it should be flaky and tender, so avoid overhandling it!) and add cold water to keep the meat filling tender and moist. The tiny details make all the difference.

1. Make the pastry: In a medium bowl, combine the flour, warm water, sunflower oil, sugar, vinegar, and salt. Using a wooden spoon and then your hands, mix and knead the dough until it is elastic and smooth, then wrap it tightly in plastic wrap and transfer to the refrigerator to rest for about half an hour.

2. While the dough is resting, make the meat filling: In a large bowl, combine the minced beef, minced onions, garlic, and cumin. Season with a pinch of salt and the pepper. While mixing everything continuously, slowly drizzle in the ice-cold water. Keep mixing the meat filling until it is sticky and smooth. Let the mixture rest in the freezer for about 10 minutes.

3. Take the dough out of the refrigerator and divide it into about 12 equal parts. Lightly dust your kitchen surface with flour and roll each piece of dough into a ball. Flatten each ball with the heel of your hand and then roll it into a thin sheet, keeping it as round as possible.

4. Place about 1½ tablespoons of the meat mixture onto one half of a dough circle and smooth it out using the back of a spoon, making sure that it stays on one side of the dough circle. Using a silicone brush dipped in water, wet the edges of the dough. Fold the other half of the

for the pastry

4¾ cups (620 grams) plain flour

1 cup (250 millilitres) warm water

1 tablespoon sunflower oil (or other neutral oil)

1 teaspoon granulated sugar

1 teaspoon apple cider vinegar

1 teaspoon coarse salt

for the meat filling

1¾ pounds (about 800 grams) minced beef

1 medium onion, peeled and finely minced

2 garlic cloves, finely minced

1 teaspoon ground cumin

Generous pinch of coarse salt and about ½ teaspoon freshly ground black pepper

1 cup minus 2 tablespoons (200 millilitres) ice-cold water

Sunflower oil (or other neutral oil), for frying

dough over the meat mixture and seal the edges shut. Using a pizza cutter or a sharp knife, trim the edges turnover to make it look like a perfect half-circle. Dip a fork in flour and press down on the edges to give them a decorative look. Repeat the process with the remaining pieces of dough and the rest of the meat mixture. Set the chibereky aside and cover them with a kitchen towel to keep the dough from drying out.

5. Heat about 3 inches (8 centimetres) of oil in a medium pan over medium-high heat until 190°C/375°F/Gas 5. Fry the chibereky one at a time until crisp and golden brown on both sides.

salamura

serves 2 to 4 | start to finish: *40 minutes*

boiled sea bass in spicy dressing   *Саламура*

The word *salamura*, which is often used in Bessarabia and the Odesa region, has two different meanings. It can refer to a spicy marinade made with salt, garlic, and fresh herbs or to the fish or vegetables that have been brined in this marinade. Here, it applies to sea bass prepared this way. I fell in love with this simple, delicious recipe and just had to share it with you. By the way, you don't have to make this dish using fish from the ocean—freshwater fish work just as well! Serve salamura with a few slices of rye bread or a light side dish such as boiled young potatoes or a salad.

1. If using whole sea bass, prep the fish: remove the head using a sharp knife, then cut off the tail and cut the rest of the fish into large chunks. Keep the tail and head in the freezer—they make a delicious fish broth. If using fillets, simply cut them into bite-size pieces.

2. Prepare the vegetables for the broth: Slice the onion into half-circles and roughly dice the carrot. Place the vegetables in a large, heavy-based saucepan, add enough cold water to submerge them completely, stir in the salt and vinegar, and bring to a boil over medium heat. Add the fish pieces and simmer everything over medium heat for about 10 minutes.

3. Make the dressing: in a small glass bowl, combine the sunflower oil and vinegar. Finely mince the dill and the garlic and add them to the mixture. If you want a spicy dressing, roughly slice the red chilli pepper and add it to the dressing. Whisk everything to combine and salt the dressing to taste.

4. Remove the fish pieces from the broth, place them in a large dish, and cover with the dressing. Let rest in the fridge for 20 minutes before serving.

for the fish

1 medium whole sea bass, about 2 pounds (1 kilogram), gutted and descaled, or 2 medium sea bass fillets
1 medium onion, peeled
1 large carrot, peeled
½ teaspoon coarse salt
¼ cup (60 millilitres) apple cider vinegar

for the salamura dressing

½ cup (125 millilitres) plus 2 tablespoons sunflower oil (or other neutral oil)
¼ cup (60 millilitres) apple cider vinegar
5 to 7 sprigs fresh dill, to taste
3 garlic cloves, peeled
1 small red chilli pepper (optional)
Coarse salt to taste

quick-pickled apples

serves 4 to 6 | start to finish: *40 minutes, plus 3 hours or overnight*

Мариновані яблука

Pickled fruit and vegetables have historically been staples of the Ukrainian diet, especially in the winter. It's not surprising—after all, how else could you have fruit and vegetables through the long cold months? But their longevity isn't the only reason pickled produce was so popular during the winter; they also go well with other traditional cold-weather dishes, such as baked duck and pork. These quick-pickled apples can be prepared any time of year, and they're also a great addition to salads (where they can be used instead of fresh apples!).

2 pounds (1 kilogram) firm, tart apples
8 cups (1.5 to 2 litres) water
¼ cup (50 grams) granulated sugar
¼ cup (60 millilitres) apple cider vinegar
2½ tablespoons coarse salt
2 garlic cloves, crushed
2 allspice berries
A few black peppercorns

1. Wash the apples, cut them into halves, and core them. Peeling them isn't necessary, but if you prefer them that way, feel free.

2. Combine the water, sugar, apple cider vinegar, and salt in a small saucepan. Bring to a boil over medium heat, stir everything to combine, and reduce the heat to a simmer. Cook the brine until the salt and sugar have fully dissolved, then take off the heat. Let the brine cool a little.

3. Place the apple halves into a clean, dry large glass jar with a screw-on lid. Add the crushed garlic cloves, the allspice, and a little black pepper. Pour the still-hot brine over the apples and fill the jar completely. Let cool to room temperature, cover with the lid, and place the pickled apples in the refrigerator. Let them pickle for a few hours or, preferably, overnight. The apples can be kept in the fridge for about a week. Before serving, drain and thinly slice the apples.

overnight pickled beetroots

Маринований буряк

makes about three 16-fluid ounce (450 milli-litres) jars	start to finish: *2 hours 20 minutes, plus overnight*

In Ukraine, families living in small villages with their own land often follow the tradition of pickling and marinating. This not only preserves the harvest but also provides delicious vegetables during the winter season. While some traditional recipes require long fermentation, not all do; pickled beetroots can be ready the next day. Prepared this way, beetroots attain a delicate texture and a pleasantly tangy flavour. They complement baked or fried fish and meat dishes perfectly and can serve as an excellent vegetarian appetizer.

2 pounds (about 1 kilogram) fresh beetroots, stems removed
4 cups (1 litre) water
2 teaspoons coarse salt
6 whole black peppercorns
6 whole cloves
3 bay leaves
1 tablespoon granulated sugar
5 tablespoons white wine vinegar

equipment: three 16-fluid ounce (450 millilitre) canning jars with new lids

1. Place the beetroots in a large saucepan with water to cover. Bring to a boil over medium-high heat and cook until tender, 20 to 30 minutes. Alternatively, you can wrap the beetroots in foil, place in an oven preheated to 190°C/375°F/Gas 5, and bake until tender, about 30 minutes.

2. While the beetroots are cooking, make the brine: add the water, salt, peppercorns, cloves, bay leaves, and sugar to a medium saucepan and bring to a rapid boil. Remove the saucepan from the heat and stir in the vinegar.

3. After the beetroots have cooked through, let them cool completely and peel off the skins. Cut the peeled beetroots in half, then slice the halves into half-moons. Transfer the slices into several clean medium-size glass jars. Pour the hot brine over the beetroots in the jars. If you're not planning on canning the beetroots, you can put the lids on the jars and keep them in the fridge for a few weeks or up to a month.

4. If you're planning on keeping the beetroots for longer, add about 4 inches (10 centimetres) of water to a large saucepan. Place the lids and the filled glass jars into the saucepan and bring the water to a boil. Reduce the heat to a simmer, carefully remove the lids, and, once they're cool enough to handle, screw them onto the jars. Add more water to fully submerge the jars, bring to a boil once more, turn off the heat, and let the jars stand in the hot water for at least 10 minutes. Carefully remove them using a potholder and let cool completely. As the lidded jars cool, they will seal—you might even hear an audible *ping* as the lids shrink a little. (**Note:** the above steps are a shortcut often used in Ukrainian cooking. For a jar sterilization process, see the note on page 12.)

5. Let the pickled beetroots rest at least overnight or for a few days before opening them—this will let the flavours meld together and intensify.

pickled cucumbers

Консервовані огірки

makes about five 16-fluid ounce (450 millilitre) jars

start to finish: *1 hour 30 minutes, plus canning time*

Preserving fresh produce by canning is a significant part of Ukrainian cuisine and traditions. Even families without their own gardens have several tried-and-true canning recipes handed down from mothers, grandmothers, and aunts. I will share my family's recipe for pickled cucumbers.

The canning season in Ukraine begins with the first harvest of vegetables grown under the open sky rather than in greenhouses. These vegetables have the best flavour when preserved in jars. It is better to use small cucumbers for preservation, as they are easier to put in jars and take out once prepared. It is important to use fresh cucumbers that have been picked within the past twenty-four hours. You can also experiment with spices and leaves. While my recipe uses bay leaves, creative Ukrainian homemakers sometimes add cherry, horseradish, or currant leaves to vary the flavour.

5 pounds (2.5 kilograms) small cucumbers
4½ cups (1.2 litres) water
1 cup (200 grams) granulated sugar
3 tablespoons coarse salt
1¼ cups (290 millilitres) white wine vinegar
10 bay leaves
1 tablespoon brown or yellow mustard seeds
10 whole black peppercorns
10 allspice berries
5 garlic cloves, peeled
10 whole cloves

equipment: five 16-fluid ounce (450 millilitre) canning jars with new lids

1. Wash the cucumbers and place them in a large bowl. Cover with cold water and let rest for at least an hour.

2. When the hour is almost up, make the brine: add the water, sugar, and salt to a small saucepan and bring it to a boil over medium-high heat. Take the saucepan off the heat and stir in the vinegar.

3. Drain the soaked cucumbers and divide them among the jars. Divide the bay leaves, mustard seeds, peppercorns, allspice berries, garlic cloves, whole cloves, and hot brine equally among the jars.

4. Add about 4 inches (10 centimetres) of water to a large saucepan. Place the lids and the filled glass jars into the saucepan and bring the water to a boil. Reduce the heat to a simmer, carefully remove the lids, and, once they're cool enough to handle, screw them onto the jars. Add more water to fully submerge the jars, bring to a boil once more, turn off the heat, and let the jars stand in the hot water for at least 10 minutes. Carefully remove the jars using a potholder and let cool completely. As the lidded jars cool, they will seal—you might even hear an audible *ping* as the lids shrink a little. (**Note:** these steps are a shortcut often used in Ukrainian cooking. For a jar sterilization process, see the note on page 12.)

5. Keep the pickles in the fridge for a few days before serving them; they will become more flavourful with each passing day.

The Authentic Ukrainian Kitchen

kvashena kapusta

ukrainian-style sauerkraut   *Квашена капуста*

serves 6 to 8   **start to finish:** *20 minutes, plus 1 week fermentation*

Kapusta is a Ukrainian superfood, sold in every grocery store and farmers' market. Despite the simplicity of its preparation, every home cook has closely guarded tips and tricks concerning the fermentation process, including the method of cutting the cabbage, the correct temperature at which to store the jars, and the fermentation time. I am sharing the simplest and most foolproof recipe.

2 medium heads cabbage,
    quartered
1 large carrot, grated
2½ tablespoons coarse salt
1 to 2 bay leaves

1. Discard the core and finely grate the cabbage using a sharp knife or mandoline.

2. In a large mixing bowl, combine the grated cabbage, the grated carrot, and the salt. Mix everything well, but try not to be too rough on the cabbage and do not squeeze the juice out of it. (Being gentle with the grated cabbage helps it remain firm and crunchy.)

3. Place the bay leaves in a very large glass jar. Tightly pack the cabbage and carrot mixture into the jar. The juices from the cabbage should cover the mixture completely. But fill the jar only two-thirds of the way up—the cabbage will expand as it ferments, so you need to leave enough space for it to do so.

4. Cover the jar with a kitchen towel or a large piece of muslin and place it in a warm, draft-free space for about a day or overnight.

5. Place a small can on a plate and press the plate down on the top of the cabbage. The juices from the cabbage might start leaking out of the jar, so place a large bowl or a towel underneath first. Leave the sauerkraut to ferment at room temperature for another few days. It might smell a little odd while it's fermenting, but trust the process.

6. After a few days, put the lid on the jar and transfer the sauerkraut to the fridge. It can be stored for a few weeks if kept very cold.

pickled tomatoes

Консервовані томати

makes 1 quart
(1 litre)

start to finish:
40 minutes

Pickled tomatoes are as popular in Ukraine as pickled cucumbers—and just as delicious. They're very tender, so don't bite into them aggressively or you may end up wearing them! Eating a pickled tomato should feel a little like kissing someone. The recipe I'm sharing here is one of the simpler and more basic ones, enhanced by dill, pepper, and a few blackcurrant leaves, which are widely used throughout the country. If you can't find the leaves, omit them, but don't be afraid to spice up the tomatoes with flavourful additions such as herbs, mustard seeds, and cloves!

If you're not planning on storing the tomatoes for long, you don't have to sterilize the jars beforehand. However, this means that you'll need to keep them in the fridge, and they'll last for only a few weeks. (See note on page 12.)

1 pound (450 grams) cherry tomatoes
Small bunch fresh dill
1 teaspoon dill seeds
A few blackcurrant leaves (optional, but they add an intriguing aroma to the pickled tomatoes)
1 teaspoon coarse salt
2 tablespoons granulated sugar
Generous pinch of freshly ground black pepper
5 tablespoons white wine vinegar

1. Wash the tomatoes and pat them dry. Place them in a sterilized glass quart (1-litre) jar (or several smaller ones) along with the dill sprigs, dill seeds, and blackcurrant leaves and set aside.

2. In a medium saucepan, combine 1⅔ cups (420 millilitres) water with the salt, sugar, and pepper. Bring the mixture to a boil, stir, and let simmer until the salt and sugar have fully dissolved. Remove the saucepan from the heat and stir in the vinegar.

3. Immediately pour the hot brine into the jar, making sure it covers all the tomatoes and herbs. After about 15 minutes, seal the jar with a lid, let the tomatoes cool to room temperature, then transfer them to a cool, dark place for a minimum of one week.

Breakfast

nalysnyky

crêpes with creamy soft cheese filling   *Налисники*

Nothing beats a thin crêpe with lots of sweet or savoury filling. Filled crêpes—whether rolled up or folded into little envelopes—are so popular in Ukraine that you can buy them ready to serve or frozen in any grocery store in the country. But while those are convenient, I'm a firm believer in making these crêpes from scratch and filling them with creamy soft cheese and sweet raisins.

1. In a small bowl, soak the raisins in hot water for about 20 minutes.

2. In a medium bowl, combine the flour with a pinch of salt and whisk to combine. In a separate small bowl, beat the eggs together with the sugar. Whisk the egg mixture into the flour, add the oil, and slowly pour in the milk, whisking as you go. The batter should be thin, so don't worry if it seems a little runny.

3. Heat an 8- or 9-inch (20- or 23-centimetre) nonstick frying pan over medium heat until sizzling and add a little oil. Using a ladle, pour a portion of the batter onto the pan. Spread it out evenly by tilting the pan to all sides and swirling the batter around. Cook the crêpe for about a minute, until the surface becomes a little bubbly and the edges start turning golden brown and crisp, then flip it over. Cook for another minute and transfer the crêpe to a large plate. Repeat the process, occasionally adding a little more oil to the pan, until you run out of batter.

4. Make the filling: In a small bowl, combine the drained raisins with the soft cheese, soured cream, sugar, and butter. Mix well. Add 2 tablespoons of the filling into the centre of each crêpe, spread it out using the back of a spoon, and fold the crêpe in half twice to make a little envelope shape. Alternatively, you can roll them up.

for the nalysnyky

1 cup (130 grams) plain flour
Pinch of coarse salt
2 large eggs
2 tablespoons granulated sugar
2 tablespoons neutral oil, plus a
    little extra for frying
1½ cups (350 millilitres) whole milk

for the filling

¼ packed cup (50 grams) raisins
1⅓ cups (300 grams) soft cheese
    or ricotta
2 tablespoons soured cream, plus
    more for serving
2 tablespoons granulated sugar
3/4 ounce (20 grams) unsalted
    butter, softened
Icing sugar, for serving (optional)

simple crêpes with honey

serves 4 | start to finish: *25 minutes*

Тонкі млинці з медом

In early spring, Ukrainians celebrate Masnytsia, or Butter Week—seven days devoted to the cooking and devouring of crêpes. But they're popular throughout the year; that's how much we like them! The secret to making perfect crêpes is finding the right recipe and having the patience to keep trying even if the first pancake (or even the first batch) turns out lumpy, uneven, or burned. Most of the time the problem is that the pan isn't hot enough, so a bad first pancake (or two!) doesn't mean there's something wrong with your batter.

1 cup (130 grams) plain flour
2 large eggs
2 tablespoons granulated sugar
Coarse salt
2 tablespoons sunflower oil (or other neutral oil)
1½ cups (350 millilitres) milk
Honey and unsalted butter, for serving

1. Sift the flour into a medium bowl. In a separate mixing bowl, combine the eggs, sugar, a pinch of salt, and the oil. Whisk until thoroughly combined. Add the flour gradually and mix well. Little by little, drizzle in the milk and mix until well combined and smooth.

2. Heat an 8- or 9-inch (20- or 23-centimetre) nonstick frying pan over medium heat until sizzling and add a little oil. Using a ladle, pour a portion of the batter onto the pan. Spread it out evenly by tilting the pan to all sides and swirling the batter around.

3. Cook for about a minute, flip the pancake, and cook for another minute. Slide the pancake onto a plate. Repeat with the remaining batter, coating the pan with more oil as needed. Serve the crêpes with honey.

lazy "varenyky" with sweet yogurt sauce

serves 4 | start to finish: *20 minutes*

soft cheese dumplings   *Ліниві вареники*

These lazy dumplings are usually given to kids, but every adult I've met loves these soft pieces of farmer-cheese-based dough as much as the average preschooler does. They're very easy to make. The main thing is to keep in mind the ratio of cheese to flour and make sure the dough feels right. If the cheese is on the moist side, you'll need to add a little more flour to the mixture. If it's a little dry, be careful not to add too much.

Note that these varenyky are not the traditional varenyky that are stuffed with various fillings; these are a shortcut version.

for the dumplings

2 cups (450 grams) soft cheese
100 grams plain flour, plus more for dusting
2 tablespoons granulated sugar
1 large egg
Pinch of coarse salt

for the sauce

1½ cups (350 millilitres) soured cream or full-fat Greek yogurt
1 tablespoon icing sugar
2 sprigs mint

1. Place the soft cheese into a sieve set over a bowl and, using the back of a spoon, push the cheese through the sieve. Work in small batches.

2. Stir the flour, sugar, egg, and a pinch of salt into the soft cheese. Mix well to combine. You should end up with a shaggy, sticky dough.

3. Fill a large saucepan with water and let it come to a boil over medium heat. Meanwhile, shape the dumplings: Transfer the cheese mixture onto a lightly floured surface, dust your hands with flour, and roll the dough out into a long sausage-like shape. Cut it into small pieces, each one roughly the size of a walnut. Shape each one into an oval and dust with a little more flour.

4. Once the water in the saucepan comes to a boil, cook the dumplings: Working in small batches, drop bits of the dough into the boiling water and wait for them to float up to the surface. As soon as they do, fish them out using a slotted spoon and transfer to a plate. (Do not overcrowd the saucepan.) Toss the cooked dumplings with a little butter to keep them from sticking together.

5. While the dumplings are cooking, make the sauce: in a small bowl, whisk together the soured cream and icing sugar until thick and smooth.

6. Serve the dumplings with a little of the sauce and garnish them with a few mint leaves.

syrnyky

serves 2 to 4 | start to finish: *40 minutes*

soft cheese pancakes   *Сирники*

If Ukrainians ever voted on their favourite breakfast dish, syrnyky—little pancakes made with soft cheese—would be the clear winner. Pretty much every Ukrainian, regardless of his or her skill in the kitchen, knows how to make this dish. Here's my favourite tried-and-true recipe (which, I am proud to say, has become the go-to recipe in many Ukrainian households!).

Syrnyky are traditionally served with soured cream or jam, but feel free to experiment with other toppings, such as maple syrup, peanut butter, and fresh fruit. You can even drizzle the pancakes with a little caramel sauce!

When you make syrnyky, your choice of soft cheese is of great importance. It should not be too dry—if it is, the syrnyky will not hold their shape well—but neither should it be too watery. If there is a lot of whey left in the cheese, you should strain it through a sieve with muslin and let the liquid drain.

2 cups (450 grams) soft cheese
1 large egg
3 tablespoons granulated sugar
1 teaspoon vanilla sugar (or a drop of vanilla extract)
Coarse salt
Plain flour, for coating
3 to 4 tablespoons sunflower oil, as needed (or other neutral oil)

1. In a large mixing bowl, combine the soft cheese, the egg, and both sugars. Add a generous pinch of salt and mix until thoroughly combined.

2. Add the flour to a large, shallow dish. Set aside.

3. Generously grease your hands with oil to keep the mixture from sticking to them. Take a heaped tablespoon of the soft cheese mixture and roll it into a ball. Dredge the ball in flour, rolling it around so that the whole surface is covered. Place the cheese ball on a plate and press it down with your hand to form a thick pancake-like shape. Repeat the process with the remaining cheese mixture.

4. Heat the remaining oil in a large frying pan over medium heat. Working in batches, place the soft cheese pancakes into the pan, keeping a little distance between them. Fry for about 3 minutes on each side or until golden brown and crispy.

5. Transfer to a large serving dish and serve with your favourite toppings.

healthy
buckwheat bowl

Боул з гречкою

serves 2 | start to finish: *30 minutes*

Traditions are great, but modern trends can capture the imagination. That is why I decided to blend the traditional and the modern in this dish. Healthy bowls with grains like quinoa have become very popular among Ukrainians, yet why should we turn to foreign cereals when we have buckwheat, a true Ukrainian tradition?

Buckwheat is believed to have originated in Asia, but Ukrainians have been cultivating and enjoying this grain since the sixteenth or seventeenth century, and this affection is reflected in our cuisine. Hrechanyky (buckwheat cutlets), lemishka (crispy flatbread), varenyky (dumplings), and pampushky (rolls) made from buckwheat flour are just a few examples that can be found in various Ukrainian cookbooks from past centuries.

Buckwheat is not only delicious but also incredibly nutritious and healthy, making it the perfect ingredient for this recipe.

½ cup plus 2 tablespoons (100 grams) toasted buckwheat groats (kasha)
2 large eggs
½ cup (75 grams) crumbled feta or other soft sheep's-milk cheese
Small bunch parsley, minced
1 medium pickle, thinly sliced
½ teaspoon dried oregano
2 to 3 tablespoons sunflower oil, to taste
Coarse salt and freshly ground black pepper to taste

1. Add 1 cup (250 millilitres) water to a small saucepan, bring it to a boil, and add the buckwheat groats. Lower the heat to a gentle simmer and cover the saucepan. Cook for about 15 minutes or until the water is mostly absorbed. Let rest, uncovered, another 5 to 10 minutes.

2. Meanwhile, make the poached eggs. Some home cooks swear by adding a little vinegar to the water; others use special appliances such as silicone bags. But my favourite (and foolproof!) technique is this: bring a large saucepan of water to a boil. Salt it generously. While the water is coming to a boil, crack an egg into a slotted spoon or a sieve placed over a small bowl or a cup and allow some of the runny egg white to drain off. Discard the drained egg white and transfer the rest of the egg into the bowl or cup. Once the water comes to a steady boil, carefully place the egg into the centre of the saucepan and lower the heat to a barely noticeable simmer. Let the egg cook 2 to 3 minutes. Using a slotted spoon, remove the egg and transfer it to a plate. Repeat the process with the second egg.

3. Once the buckwheat has cooked through and the poached eggs are ready, assemble the bowl: scoop the buckwheat into one side of the bowl and arrange the crumbled feta, minced parsley, and sliced pickle on the other side. Place the poached egg on top of the buckwheat, sprinkle everything with a little oregano, and drizzle some oil over the egg. Salt and season with freshly ground black pepper to taste.

goat's cheese and herb oatmeal

serves 2

start to finish:
20 minutes

Вівсянка з сиром та травами

While porridge is not a traditional Ukrainian breakfast dish, it has gained incredible popularity over the past few decades. While most Ukrainians prefer sweet porridge, I am a fan of this savoury recipe with crumbly bryndza cheese and fragrant herbs.

Bryndza cheese has a diverse historical background. Traditionally, Hutsuls (an ethnic group of western Ukraine) engaged in sheep farming, and they crafted this cheese right in the meadows. Authentic Hutsul bryndza is made from sheep's milk, though variations made from cow's or goat's milk have also emerged. For this recipe, I recommend using goat's cheese, as it has a distinct flavour and is affordable.

1¼ cups (275 millilitres) water
¾ cup (100 grams) instant porridge oats
2 ½ ounces (45 grams) unsalted butter
1 pinch of dried oregano
1 pinch of dried thyme
⅓ cup (50 grams) soft goat's cheese
Coarse salt to taste

1. Bring the water to a boil in a small saucepan over medium heat and add the oats. Reduce the heat and cook the oats, stirring from time to time, for 1 or 2 minutes or until they have softened and the mixture has thickened into a porridge.

2. Take the saucepan off the heat and transfer the porridge to a serving bowl. Stir in the butter, garnish with the dried herbs, and crumble the goat's cheese on top. Season to taste. Serve hot!

pumpkin porridge with millet

Гарбузова каша з пшоном

Millet has been a staple of Ukrainian cuisine since ancient times. Perhaps one of the most common dishes is Millet Kulish (page 157), which was very popular during the time of the Cossacks. Another is kachana kasha, made from millet, eggs, and flour, a specialty from the Poltava region.

During the Soviet era, Ukrainians rarely used millet due to the poor quality and not-so-great taste of the Soviets' product. Later, after Ukraine's independence, foreign grains like rice, bulgur, and quinoa took over.

Now millet is making a comeback. People are learning how to cook it deliciously and appreciate its nutritional value.

One of the most popular millet dishes today is pumpkin porridge, which can be made with either raw or canned pumpkin. Just make sure the texture of the dish is nice and even.

While cinnamon is not a traditional Ukrainian spice, it adds an incredible flavour twist to this dish.

1 cup (200 grams) millet
4 cups (1 litre) milk
¼ cup (50 grams) granulated sugar
1 cinnamon stick
Large pinch of coarse salt
1 pound (450 grams) pumpkin, peeled and roughly cubed
3½ ounces (100 grams) unsalted butter

1. Thoroughly rinse the millet several times until the water runs clear. If you're in a hurry, you can rinse it once using hot water instead of cold—this will get rid of the slightly bitter aftertaste that can linger if you haven't rinsed the grains well enough. Transfer the millet to a medium saucepan and add the milk, sugar, cinnamon stick, and a generous pinch of salt. Add the cubed pumpkin and half the butter, bring to a gentle simmer, and cook everything over low heat for about 20 minutes, stirring occasionally.

2. While the porridge is cooking, preheat the oven to 180°C/350°F/Gas 4.

3. Take the saucepan off the heat and remove the cinnamon stick. Stir everything well to combine. Transfer the half-cooked porridge to a baking dish and place the remaining butter on top of the porridge. Place it in the preheated oven and bake for 30 minutes.

4. After the porridge is done (the chunks of pumpkin should be tender and the porridge should be nice and thick), take it out of the oven and let cool a little. Serve warm.

manna kasha

serves 2 | start to finish: *20 minutes*

semolina porridge with hempseed oil and hemp seeds

Манна каша з насінням і олією конопель

Semolina porridge—known as manna kasha—has a questionable reputation in Ukraine, as it's mostly associated with bland school meals in Soviet-era kindergartens. But I'm convinced that the people who don't like it have never had good versions of this dish, which is a porridge similar to grits in the U.S. and polenta in Italy but made with wheat.

Instead of adding copious amounts of sugar, as is customary, I make a savoury version with hempseed oil and hemp seeds, which are a staple of Ukrainian cuisine. For a long time, hempseed oil and toasted hemp seeds were quite popular in Ukraine and across the entire Eurasian continent. However, hempseed oil lost its popularity in the early twentieth century, partly due to the reputation of cannabis, with which hemp was associated, and partly due to stiff competition from sunflowers.

If you can't find hempseed oil and hemp seeds for this recipe, replace them with unrefined sunflower oil and sunflower seeds.

3½ ounces (100 grams) semolina
2 cups plus 2 tablespoons (530 millilitres) low-fat milk
Coarse salt and freshly ground black pepper to taste
2 tablespoons hempseed oil
2 tablespoons unhulled hemp seeds

1. In a medium saucepan over medium heat, toast the semolina until golden brown and fragrant. Stir while toasting so that the semolina doesn't burn.

2. Slowly pour in the milk, stir well to combine everything (pay extra attention to the bottom of the saucepan and the corners!), reduce heat to low, and cook, stirring continuously, for a few minutes or until the cereal thickens.

3. Take the saucepan off the heat and season with salt and freshly ground black pepper to taste. Divide the cereal between two bowls, drizzle each portion with a little hempseed oil, and garnish with the hemp seeds. Serve hot!

fried eggs with tomatoes and spring onions

Яєчня з томатами і цибулею

In Ukraine, the second-most-popular breakfast after Syrnyky (page 70) is fried eggs. The simplest and most common way to serve them is with pan-fried tomatoes and onions. Here, I enhance the taste with fresh spring onions, which complement the dish perfectly.

2 tablespoons sunflower oil
1 small onion, sliced
1 medium tomato, cored and sliced
4 large eggs
Coarse salt and freshly ground
    black pepper
2 spring onions, finely chopped
Crusty bread, for serving

1. Heat the oil in a medium frying pan over medium-high heat. Sauté the onion slices until fragrant and lightly golden.

2. After a few minutes, add the tomato slices to the pan and cook, stirring from time to time, for a minute or two.

3. Crack the eggs into the pan. Reduce the heat to low and fry the eggs for 4 to 5 minutes or until your desired level of doneness. Salt the eggs and sprinkle a little freshly ground pepper on top of the yolks. Garnish the eggs with the spring onions. Serve with a little crusty bread to dip in the egg yolk.

fried potatoes with goat's cheese and garlic

Смажена картопля з сиром і часником

The first mention of potatoes in Europe was in the sixteenth century. According to one theory, they were brought by the Spanish from South America. However, it was not until the early nineteenth century that potatoes were grown specifically for human consumption in Ukraine. This cultivation began in the Kharkiv region. Over the centuries, we've learned not only how to grow an abundance of this root vegetable but also how to cook it to perfection. Pan-fried potatoes are an obvious favourite, both in my book and in households across Ukraine. In some regions of the country, they are traditionally served with a little crumbly goat's cheese and some fragrant garlic. Heavenly!

1¾ pounds (800 grams) potatoes, peeled
2 garlic cloves, peeled
2 tablespoons sunflower oil
Coarse salt and freshly ground black pepper to taste
1 cup (110 grams) crumbled goat's cheese

1. Cut the potatoes into thin wedges or thick slices, depending on your preference. Keep in mind that the thicker the slices, the longer they take to cook. Set the potatoes aside. Crush and finely mince the garlic cloves.

2. Heat the oil in a large frying pan over medium heat. Arrange the potato slices in one layer and season them with salt and pepper. Cook, undisturbed, for about 5 minutes or until the bottoms are golden and crusty. Flip the potatoes and cook for 5 more minutes, making sure they don't burn. Add the minced garlic and cook everything for a few more minutes, until the potatoes are crumbly and the garlic is fragrant. Remove the pan from the heat and transfer the potatoes to a large serving dish.

3. Sprinkle the crumbled goat's cheese over the potatoes. If needed, add a little more salt and black pepper to taste.

Salads

baked cabbage, tomato, and chicken salad

serves 2 | start to finish: *50 minutes*

Салат з запеченою капустою, томатами і куркою

Dishes made from oven-baked vegetables can be found in many ancient Ukrainian cookbooks. This is unsurprising, because this method of cooking leaves the ingredients flavourful and highlights their complexity. This recipe for baked cabbage salad is incredibly simple and delicious, and the addition of chicken breasts makes it into a meal.

1. Preheat the oven to 220°C/425°F/Gas 7.

2. Core the cabbage and cut it into quarters. Drizzle a tablespoon of oil into an ovenproof dish and lay out the cabbage pieces. Cut the lemon into halves and squeeze the juice from one of the halves over the cabbage. Set the other half aside—it will be used to make the mayonnaise. Season the cabbage with salt and drizzle a little more oil over it.

3. Bake in the preheated oven for 25 to 30 minutes or until the edges turn dark brown and crispy.

4. Meanwhile, prep the chicken breasts: if needed, trim off the excess fat; season with a little salt and cut into thin strips.

5. In a small bowl, make the marinade: whisk together 2 tablespoons oil, the ground paprika, and the mustard and set aside. Transfer the chicken strips to a medium bowl and add the marinade. Using your hands, massage the marinade into the chicken. Cover the bowl with plastic wrap and let rest in the fridge for about 20 minutes.

6. Remove the chicken strips from the fridge and pat dry with kitchen paper. Heat a little sunflower oil in a medium pan over medium heat. Add the chicken strips and sear them until golden on all sides and cooked through.

7. While the chicken is cooking, make the mayonnaise: In a clean, dry bowl, whisk together the egg yolk, the mustard, and the juice from the second lemon half. Whisking continuously, slowly drizzle in the sunflower oil until thick. Salt the mayonnaise to taste and set aside.

8. Arrange the baked cabbage pieces on a large serving dish. Core and quarter the tomatoes and arrange them alongside the cabbage. Lay the cooked chicken on top of the vegetables and generously drizzle everything with the homemade mayonnaise.

½ medium head white cabbage
3 tablespoons sunflower oil
1 medium lemon
Coarse salt
2 medium chicken breasts, skinless and boneless (about ¾ pound/350 grams total)
1 teaspoon ground paprika
1 teaspoon mustard
3 to 4 tablespoons homemade mayonnaise (recipe below), to taste
2 medium tomatoes

for the homemade mayonnaise

1 large egg yolk
1 teaspoon good-quality mustard
3 to 4 tablespoons sunflower oil
Coarse salt to taste

new potatoes with dill and bacon

Молода картопля з кропом і салом

If there's anything Ukrainians like more than regular potatoes, it's *baby* potatoes. Their annual arrival in grocery stores and farmers' markets across the country is something of a national celebration. They even look special, all clean and rosy.

It doesn't take much work to make this root vegetable really shine. Just boil them whole and serve with a little butter and some finely minced dill, and you'll have a dinner fit for a gourmet. But if you want something even more mouthwatering, fry up some nice, crispy bacon to go along with the pillowy new potatoes.

1 pound (450 grams) small new potatoes, scrubbed clean but not peeled
Coarse salt and freshly ground black pepper
Small bunch fresh dill
A few slices of bacon
2⅛ ounces (60 unsalted butter)
1 to 2 tablespoons white wine vinegar, to taste

1. Place the whole, unpeeled potatoes into a large saucepan, add enough water to fully cover them, salt it generously, and bring to a boil over medium heat. Reduce the heat and cook at a low simmer for about 20 minutes or until you can pierce the potatoes easily with a knife. The cooking time will depend on the size of your potatoes.

2. Meanwhile, finely mince the dill and set it aside. In a medium frying pan over medium heat, cook the bacon to your desired level of crispness. Remove it from the pan and transfer it to a kitchen-paper-lined plate to absorb excess fat.

3. Once the potatoes are done, drain them and return them to the saucepan. Add the butter and the minced dill and toss the potatoes to cover them in the melted butter and herbs. Add the vinegar, toss everything once more, and let the potatoes rest in the saucepan for about 10 minutes.

4. Transfer the potatoes to a large serving plate, garnish with the bacon slices, and season to taste. Serve warm!

easy
carrot and
apple salad

Салат з моркви та яблука

It is difficult to imagine a more flavourful combination of fresh vegetables and fruits than this simple salad. Salads made with both boiled and raw carrots are found in century-old Ukrainian cookbooks. I highlight the carrot flavour with an equally tasty and healthy apple as well as fragrant spices.

In a medium mixing bowl, combine the apples and carrot, season them with salt and the ground coriander seeds, and drizzle with the oil. Mix until everything is well combined, adjust seasoning to taste, and serve.

2 large tart apples (such as Granny Smith), peeled and cut into fine matchsticks
1 large carrot, peeled and cut into fine matchsticks
1 teaspoon coarse salt
1 teaspoon ground coriander seeds
3 tablespoons unrefined sunflower oil

cucumber, mint, and celery salad

Салат з огірка, м'яти та селери

Fresh cucumbers and herbs are my go-to summer salad. Cucumbers may be available in your market year-round, but they taste best when they're in season. Take every opportunity to add them to your summer diet. Many people make this salad with fresh dill, but I prefer to use fresh mint, which adds a uniquely fresh flavour.

5 medium cucumbers, thinly sliced
2 stalks celery, thinly sliced
2 tablespoons unrefined sunflower
   oil
Juice of 1 lemon
Coarse salt to taste
4 sprigs mint (only the leaves)

1. Place the sliced cucumbers and celery in a mixing bowl.

2. Drizzle the vegetables with the sunflower oil and add the lemon juice. Add a generous pinch of salt and toss everything to combine.

3. Transfer the salad to a serving plate and garnish with the mint leaves.

cucumber, spring onion, egg, and radish salad

Салат з яйцем, огірком, редисом та зеленою цибулею

Salads such as this one appear on the tables of Ukrainian families in the spring, when the farmers' markets are full of young vegetables. It is a kind of tradition to start spring by making this salad, which, like many Ukrainian salads, is dressed with aromatic oil and does not necessarily include a strong acidic component like a vinaigrette. Here, I chose a dressing of fragrant sunflower oil, but many people like soured cream. They are equally delicious.

1. Thinly slice the cucumber and radishes, add them to a medium bowl, and set aside.

2. Cut the eggs into quarters and set them aside.

3. Finely chop the spring onions and add them to the cucumber and radish slices.

4. Drizzle the salad with oil, mix everything well to combine, and garnish with the quartered eggs. Season to taste with salt and freshly ground black pepper.

1 medium cucumber
3 medium radishes
2 hard-boiled eggs, peeled
3 spring onions, white part discarded
3 tablespoons unrefined sunflower oil
Coarse salt and freshly ground black pepper

baked root vegetable salad

Салат з запечених коренеплодів

serves 4

start to finish:
*1 hour
30 minutes*

Oven-roasted vegetables are a staple of Ukrainian cuisine, especially during the colder months and until the new harvest. You can roast anything: celery, beetroots, carrots, pumpkin. We turn them into purées or simply add them as side dishes to meat or fish.

I decided to try combining all of them into one delicious and vibrantly coloured salad, and the result exceeded all my expectations!

1. Preheat the oven to 180°C/350°F/Gas 4 and line a baking sheet with baking paper.

2. Cut the beetroots, pumpkin, carrots and onions into large chunks and arrange them in a single layer on the baking sheet. Drizzle with a little oil and bake in the preheated oven for about 50 minutes or until the vegetables are tender enough to be easily pierced by a fork.

3. Meanwhile, toast the sunflower and pumpkin seeds in a dry pan over medium heat until fragrant.

4. Once the vegetables have cooked through, remove them from the oven. Let them cool a little and then peel the beetroot chunks. Transfer the vegetables to a large mixing dish, drizzle with the lemon juice, season, and garnish with the toasted seeds and rosemary leaves.

½ pound (225 grams) beetroots, washed but unpeeled
½ pound (225 grams) pumpkin, peeled and seeded
½ pound (225 grams) carrots, peeled
2 medium red onions, peeled
1 tablespoon unrefined sunflower oil
1 tablespoon sunflower seeds
1 tablespoon pumpkin seeds
1 tablespoon lemon juice
Coarse salt and freshly ground black pepper to taste
1 sprig rosemary

tomato, cucumber, and onion salad

Салат з томатами, огірками та цибулею

Cooking doesn't have to be expensive, time-consuming, or difficult. Sometimes it's all about the simple time-tested recipes that don't take long to prepare and taste heavenly, like this tomato, cucumber, and onion salad. Just make sure the vegetables are in season—you want perfectly crunchy cucumbers and ripe, sweet tomatoes. I use unrefined sunflower oil as a simple dressing here, but you can also try tossing the vegetables with a little soured cream.

1 large red onion, peeled
3 medium cucumbers, cut in half lengthwise, then thickly sliced
3 large tomatoes, diced
3 to 4 tablespoons unrefined sunflower oil, to taste
Coarse salt and freshly ground black pepper to taste

1. Thinly slice the red onion and set aside.

2. Combine all the vegetables in a large mixing bowl. Add the sunflower oil, salt, and black pepper and toss to combine.

tsvikli

traditional beetroot and horseradish salad　　*Цвіклі*

I joke that Ukrainians have beetroot juice flowing through their veins instead of blood. In addition to many, many kinds of borsch, Ukrainian cuisine is rich in other beetroot-based dishes, like this simple relish. It goes perfectly with both meat and fish as a condiment. Or just put a thin piece of salo on bread, add a generous helping of tsvikli on top, and prepare to have your taste buds blown away by the flavour.

1. To cook the beetroots, either wrap them in foil and roast them in a 200°C/400°F/Gas 6 oven for 50 to 60 minutes or simmer them in a large saucepan of lightly salted water for 20 to 40 minutes. The cooking time will depend on the size of the beetroots, so make sure to check on them every 20 minutes or so. They are cooked through when they can be pierced easily with a fork.

2. Let the cooked beetroots cool until they can be comfortably handled. Using a sharp paring knife or a vegetable peeler, peel off the skins. Using a box grater, finely grate the cooked beetroots, transfer them to a medium bowl, and set aside.

3. Grate the horseradish root and add it to the bowl with the grated beetroots. In a separate small bowl, combine the vinegar, sugar, and salt. Add the dressing to the beetroots and the horseradish and mix everything to combine. If needed, adjust the seasoning to taste.

2 pounds (900 grams) beetroots, washed but unpeeled
1 small (2- to 3-inch, about 100 grams) piece fresh horseradish root, peeled
2 tablespoons apple cider vinegar or lemon juice
1 teaspoon granulated sugar
1 teaspoon coarse salt

simple cabbage salad with dill

Салат з капустою та кропом

Time and again, Ukrainian cooks show that the most delicious dishes can also be the simplest to prepare, especially when they're made with love and fresh, seasonal produce. This wonderful salad comes together in a pinch from just a handful of easy-to-find ingredients, and with a few adjustments (such as using a fall or summer variety of cabbage), it can be made in any season. It's delicate and fresh if you use young cabbage in the spring and slightly crunchier if you make it with fall cabbage. And if you really want to highlight its taste, be sure to use cold-pressed, unfiltered (unrefined) sunflower oil.

½ medium head white cabbage, cored
5 sprigs dill
Coarse salt
2 tablespoons distilled white vinegar
2 tablespoons unrefined sunflower oil

1. Using a large, sharp knife, finely chop the cabbage, then transfer it to a large mixing bowl and set aside. Finely mince the dill and sprinkle it over the cabbage. Add a generous pinch of salt and mix everything to combine.

2. Add the vinegar and the sunflower oil and mix everything until well combined. If needed, adjust seasoning to taste.

tomato and oyster mushroom salad

Салат з томатами та гливами

serves 2 | start to finish: *15 minutes*

Dishes with wild mushrooms are very popular in the Carpathian region of Ukraine. Wild mushrooms are salted, fermented, dried, and added to meat dishes and soups or made into delicious salads. But the wild-mushroom season passes far too quickly, so I make a salad using oyster mushrooms, which are similar in consistency and taste to wild mushrooms but are more readily available.

½ pound (225 grams) oyster mushrooms, stems removed
2 tablespoons sunflower oil
Coarse salt and freshly ground black pepper to taste
Small bunch parsley
½ pound (225 grams) tomatoes
½ cup (100 grams) soft cheese

1. Roughly chop the oyster mushrooms. In a small frying pan, heat half the oil over medium heat and sauté the mushrooms for about 3 minutes or until golden on all sides. Season to taste with salt and freshly ground pepper.

2. Mince the parsley and set aside. Quarter the tomatoes and combine them in a large mixing bowl with the minced parsley. Stir in the soft cheese and add the fried oyster mushrooms. Drizzle with the remaining oil and add salt and pepper to taste.

Soup & Borsch

rybna yushka

traditional fish soup   *Рибна юшка*

The word *yushka* is often used to denote any kind of soup (except borsch). These soups are traditionally made with local ingredients such as vegetables and fish that can be found in the lakes and rivers of Ukraine and in the Black Sea. Each region (if not each household!) has its own special yushka recipe. This is my take on this iconic dish; in it, I decided to use butter, which makes the taste especially delicate.

1. Cut the fish fillets into bite-size pieces and set aside. Roughly dice the potatoes and set them aside.

2. Make the vegetable broth: wash and peel the parsley root and carrots and roughly dice them. Wash the onion and celeriac and cut them into quarters. Toast the vegetables in a dry pan over medium heat until you get a little colour on them. Take the pan off the heat and transfer the vegetables to a large saucepan. Add enough water to cover the vegetables and bring to a boil over medium heat. Reduce the heat and add the bay leaves and allspice. Simmer for about 30 minutes.

3. Meanwhile, make the tomato base: if using fresh tomatoes, grate them with a box grater and set aside. If using canned tomatoes, roughly chop them. Heat the butter in a medium saucepan over medium heat and add the grated or chopped tomatoes. Simmer for about 10 minutes or until most of the liquid has evaporated. Add the cognac, simmer for a few more minutes, and remove from the heat.

4. Stir the cooked tomatoes into the vegetable broth. Add the diced potatoes, parsley (stems removed), fish pieces, and coriander seeds. After about 20 minutes, remove and discard the celeriac and the onion. Add the garlic clove, simmer for a few minutes more, and remove from the heat. Season to taste with salt and freshly ground pepper before serving.

1½ pounds (680 grams) whitefish fillets (any freshwater fish)
3 medium potatoes
1 whole parsley root or medium parsnip
2 large carrots
1 large onion
¼ celeriac, trimmed and peeled
3 bay leaves
8 allspice berries
3 tomatoes (or half a 14-ounce/400-gram can peeled tomatoes)
2⅛ ounces (60 grams) unsalted butter
3 tablespoons cognac or brandy
1 bunch parsley
1 teaspoon coriander seeds
1 garlic clove
Coarse salt and freshly ground black pepper to taste

kalatusha

serves 4 to 6 | start to finish: *1 hour 30 minutes*

creamy fish soup with mushrooms   *Калатуша*

Sometimes Ukrainian cuisine catches you off guard with its unusual combinations of ingredients, and this soup, which comes from the Chernihiv region, is an example. The base of the soup is mushrooms and fish (usually carp or other freshwater fish). What sets kalatusha apart is that it is thickened with flour fried in butter, giving the soup a pleasant silky texture.

In this recipe, I used pollock, which you can probably find in any store, but you can also try carp, zander, or pike.

1. Preheat the oven to 190°C/375°F/Gas 5. If using dried porcini mushrooms, soak them in a small bowl of cold water for about 15 minutes.

2. Dice the celeriac and slice one of the carrots into thick slices. Transfer them to a baking dish, drizzle with about a teaspoon of oil, cover with foil, and bake in the preheated oven for about 40 minutes or until tender enough to be pierced with a fork. Transfer the cooked vegetables into a blender and blitz until smooth, adding a little water or oil if the mixture is too thick.

3. Slice the remaining carrot and add the slices to a medium saucepan. Peel the onion, cut it in half, and add it to the saucepan. Cover with cold water, add the drained dried mushrooms (or the cleaned fresh mushrooms), garlic cloves, bay leaves, and allspice. Bring to a boil over medium heat. Cut the fish fillets into bite-size pieces, add them to the broth, reduce the heat, and cook everything for 20 to 25 minutes.

4. Make the roux: toast the flour in a small saucepan over medium heat until golden, then add the butter. Once the butter has melted, whisk the mixture into a smooth paste.

5. Filter the mushroom and fish broth through a sieve. Discard the onion and spices, finely chop the other ingredients, and set them aside. Transfer the filtered broth back into the saucepan and slowly whisk in the roux until the soup thickens.

6. Ladle the soup into deep bowls, add a heaped spoonful of the carrot-and-celery purée into the centre of each dish, and garnish with a little of the chopped-up mushrooms and fish. Arrange the sprigs of dill on top. If needed, season everything to taste.

½ pound (225 grams) fresh or frozen porcini mushrooms (or ¼ cup/30 grams dried porcini mushrooms)
1 whole celeriac, trimmed and peeled
2 large carrots
3 tablespoons sunflower oil
1 large onion
2 garlic cloves
2 bay leaves
5 allspice berries
1 small Alaskan pollock fillet (about 1 pound/450 grams)
3 tablespoons plain flour
2¾ ounces (75 grams) unsalted butter
3 sprigs dill, for garnishing
Coarse salt and freshly ground black pepper to taste

kapusnyak

sauerkraut soup   *Капусняк*

Adding fermented vegetables to the first course of a meal is common in Ukrainian cuisine, and one of the most popular pickled-vegetable dishes is sauerkraut soup. It might sound a little odd, but trust me—it's absolutely breathtaking. It's also incredibly easy to make, so you can prepare this soup every week throughout the cold season.

Combining the sauerkraut with the pork is the key. The sourness balances out the fat, enhancing the taste of the dish. Many Ukrainian cooks make a version of kapusnyak with fresh cabbage. To try it, just replace half the sauerkraut with grated fresh cabbage.

1 pound (450 grams) boneless
   pork shoulder
1 bay leaf
2 allspice berries
1 large carrot
1 large onion
2 tablespoons sunflower oil
2½ cups (350 grams) sauerkraut
5 medium starchy potatoes
Coarse salt and freshly ground
   pepper

1. Cut the pork shoulder into bite-size pieces and put them in a medium saucepan. Add enough cold water to completely cover the meat and bring to a rapid boil over medium heat. Reduce the heat and cook at a simmer for about 1 hour, occasionally skimming off and discarding the foam. After an hour, add the bay leaf and the allspice and continue cooking over low heat.

2. While the broth is simmering, grate the carrot using a box grater. Peel and dice the onion. Add a little oil to a saucepan placed over medium heat and sauté the grated carrot and the diced onion until fragrant. Add the sauerkraut. Ladle some of the broth into the pan so the vegetables don't dry out. Once the vegetables are tender, take the pan off the heat.

3. Peel and dice the potatoes and add them to the broth. Simmer for about 20 minutes and then add the sautéed vegetables to the saucepan. Bring everything to a rapid boil, reduce the heat, simmer the soup for about 5 minutes, and remove from the heat. Season with a little salt and freshly ground pepper and let rest a little before serving.

borsch with pork ribs and smoked pears

Борщ на свинячих ребрах з копченою грушею

Borsch isn't just a traditional dish in Ukraine—it's a national symbol. In fact, I'd go so far as to say it is part of our cultural DNA. But don't worry, there's no right or wrong way to make this iconic dish. Each Ukrainian family has its own special borsch recipe lovingly passed down over generations.

Of the many recipes I've gathered over the years, this is one of my favourites—the aroma of the smoked pears really highlights the rich flavour of the meat and the delicate vegetables. Dried and smoked pears, along with other dried fruits, are used to prepare Uzvar (page 247), a traditional Ukrainian drink. However, the flavour of smoked pears also wonderfully complements borsch and is an essential ingredient in some recipes. If you do not have smoked pears on hand, you can try adding a bit of smoked prunes to your borsch.

Whatever you do, don't say borsch is "just a soup"—if you do, you'll definitely get a few angry looks from Ukrainians.

1. Preheat the oven to 200°C/400°F/Gas 6.

2. In an ovenproof dish, bake the pork ribs for about 30 minutes or until a golden crust forms. (If you prefer, you can fry the ribs in a dry pan over medium heat instead.) Meanwhile, roughly chop the celeriac and the carrots. Transfer the baked ribs to a large saucepan and add about 105 fluid ounces (3 litres) water. Add the celeriac and carrot chunks and half an unpeeled onion. Bring the water to a rapid boil, lower the heat, and let simmer over medium heat for about 30 minutes.

3. Meanwhile, make the sautéed-vegetable base, the aromatic foundation of the borsch: Finely cut the pepper into matchsticks. Finely dice the tomatoes. Peel and thinly slice the remaining half of the onion.

4. Heat the butter in a large frying pan, add the vegetables, and cook them until soft and fragrant. Stir in the tomato purée and simmer everything for another 5 to 7 minutes.

5. Using a box grater, grate one of the beetroots. Add it to the sautéed vegetables and cook everything for another 3 to 4 minutes. While the vegetables are cooking, dice the potatoes roughly and add them to the saucepan with the rib broth. Add the garlic to the saucepan.

1 pound (450 grams) pork ribs
¼ celeriac, washed and trimmed
2 medium carrots, peeled
1 onion, unpeeled
1 pepper, cored
2 large tomatoes
½ ounce (15 grams) unsalted
    butter
¼ cup (60 grams)
    tomato purée
2 whole beetroots, peeled
4 medium potatoes, peeled
2 to 3 garlic cloves, to taste,
    crushed and peeled
2 bay leaves
3 allspice berries
Coarse salt to taste
One 14-ounce (400-gram) can
    white beans (optional)
¼ head of cabbage
1 to 2 smoked dried pears, to taste
    (or use
    a teaspoon of smoked paprika)
Sprigs of fresh dill and soured
    cream for serving

recipe continues

6. Using a food processor with a juicing attachment, squeeze the juice out of the remaining beetroot (alternatively, you can simply grate it using the fine holes on your box grater and then squeeze the juice through a sieve). Add the beetroot juice, the sautéed vegetables, the bay leaves, and the allspice to the saucepan with the ribs and celery. Salt to taste. If you like, you can add a can of precooked white beans to the borsch at this point.

7. Grate or finely chop the cabbage and set it aside. (It will not be added to the borsch until just before everything else is done; if you add it earlier, it will come out too mushy.) Add the smoked dried pears (or the smoked paprika) to the saucepan.

8. Once all the ingredients have cooked through and are tender, add the grated cabbage to the saucepan. Simmer for 5 more minutes, then take the saucepan off the heat. Let the borsch rest for at least half an hour. Before serving, garnish with soured cream and finely chopped dill. Save extra borsch in the fridge and keep in mind that it tastes best on the second day, when the flavours have had time to meld and intensify.

vegetarian borsch with lekvar

(Carpathian plum butter)   *Овочевий борщ з лекваром*

We often think of borsch as a meat-based dish, but vegetarian options are widely popular and just as authentic as borsch with pork ribs or beef. In certain regions of Ukraine—for example, Poltava Oblast—a thick plum butter called lekvar is traditionally added to vegetable borsch. The tangy sweetness of the plums balances out the taste of the borsch and makes it even richer and more velvety.

This and other vegetarian versions of borsch were most often prepared by Ukrainians during religious fasting periods when meat was not eaten. These versions of borsch could include, in addition to lekvar, fresh or pickled tomatoes, fresh or dried wild mushrooms, and even aubergines.

And although making lekvar is simple enough, you can use store-bought jam and whip up a delicious traditional borsch in less than an hour.

1. Make the lekvar: place about ½ pound (225 grams) of pitted plums in a small saucepan and add 2 cups (500 millilitres) of cold water. Bring the mixture to a low boil over medium heat and reduce heat to a simmer. Cook the plums until soft, drain excess water, and add everything to a food processor. Blend until smooth, then transfer the mixture back to the saucepan, stir in sugar to taste, and cook over low heat until the plum butter thickens. Lekvar can be stored in an airtight glass jar in the fridge for one to two weeks.

2. Make the broth: fill a large, heavy-based pot with about 10 cups (2.5 litres) water. Add 1 whole beetroot, 1 whole carrot, 1 whole onion, and the celeriac. Bring to a simmer and cook over medium heat for about 40 minutes. Add a few allspice berries and the bay leaf.

3. While the broth is cooking, peel and finely chop the remaining onion and cook it in sunflower oil until tender, fragrant, and translucent. Peel and grate the remaining beetroot and carrot and add them to the pan. After a few minutes, add the tomato purée and about ½ cup (120 millilitres) of the vegetable broth.

4. Remove the vegetables and bay leaf from the broth. Add the diced potatoes to the saucepan and bring to a simmer. Cook the potatoes until tender. Salt the broth to taste.

recipe continues

for the lekvar

4 or 5 pitted plums (about ½ pound/225 grams)
2 cups (500 millilitres) water
Granulated sugar to taste

for the borsch

2 whole beetroots, scrubbed
2 whole carrots, scrubbed
2 medium onions
½ celeriac, scrubbed
A few allspice berries
1 bay leaf
Sunflower oil (or other neutral oil)
2 tablespoons tomato purée
4 firm medium potatoes, peeled and diced
Coarse salt to taste
¼ head of a medium cabbage, cored
½ red pepper, cut into matchsticks
1 to 2 garlic cloves, to taste
Soured cream and fresh parsley, for garnishing (optional)

5. Using a sharp knife, grate the cored cabbage into thin strips. Add the cabbage to the saucepan with the potatoes and broth. Bring everything to a boil and reduce the heat to a simmer.

6. Add the pepper to the sautéed vegetables. Sauté everything until tender but not overcooked, adding more broth as necessary. Once the sautéed vegetables are tender, add them to the broth and bring everything to a brief boil once again. Reduce to a simmer. Stir in 1 to 2 tablespoons of lekvar.

7. Crush and peel the garlic cloves. Add them to the saucepan. Simmer everything for 5 more minutes and take off the heat. Serve hot (although borsch is also great the next day; after it has had a chance to rest, the taste intensifies even more). Garnish with soured cream and fresh parsley (optional).

green borsch

Зелений борщ

As soon as vegetables begin to grow in the spring, Ukrainians start making green borsch. To be fair, green borsch doesn't have much in common with the vibrant red dish you're probably imagining; it doesn't even have beetroots in it! But the two hearty stews do have things in common—the love Ukrainians have for them and the fact that every household has its own recipe.

2 large onions, peeled
1 medium carrot, peeled and halved
¼ celeriac, peeled and cut into large chunks
2 to 3 bay leaves, to taste
4 allspice berries
3 tablespoons sunflower oil
4 large potatoes, scrubbed clean and peeled
3 large eggs
Coarse salt
1 bunch sorrel (or about 3 cups/700 grams fresh spinach)
1 bunch nettles (or about 3 cups/700 grams fresh spinach)
1 bunch spring onions
1 bunch flat-leaf parsley

1. Add 1 onion to a saucepan and cover with water. Add 1 carrot half, the chunks of celeriac, the bay leaves, and the allspice berries to the saucepan; bring to a boil and cook over low heat for about 30 minutes. Remove and discard the vegetables.

2. Finely dice the second onion and sauté it in the sunflower oil in a medium frying pan over medium heat until soft and fragrant. Grate the remaining carrot half and add it to the pan. Sauté the onion and carrot together for about 5 minutes.

3. Cube the peeled potatoes and add them to the saucepan with the vegetable broth. Simmer for 15 minutes.

4. Place the eggs in a small saucepan or pot, cover with cold water, salt generously, and bring to a boil. Cook them for 5 to 7 minutes, then drain and douse with cold water—this will make them easier to peel.

5. Finely mince the sorrel, nettles, spring onions, and parsley. Add them to the saucepan. Bring everything to a rapid boil and turn off the heat. Salt the borsch to taste.

6. Serve hot, adding half a hard-boiled egg to each bowl.

hrybna yushka

serves 4 to 6 | start to finish:
1 hour
15 minutes

mushroom soup   *Грибна юшка*

As mentioned on page 113, in Ukraine, *yushka* refers to any soup other than borsch, including soups prepared with vegetables, fish, or even game meat. In the Carpathian Mountains, where mushrooms are a staple, mushroom yushka has long been a favourite. Various edible mushrooms are traditionally used, among them chanterelles, honey fungus, and, the most delicious choice, porcini. Over time, mushroom yushka gained popularity in other regions of Ukraine. Nowadays, it's often made with common button mushrooms, sometimes in combination with fresh or dried wild mushrooms.

1. Make the vegetable broth: peel and roughly chop 1 of the carrots; peel and halve 1 of the onions; and chop the celery stalk into bite-size chunks. Put the vegetables in a saucepan, add enough cold water to cover them completely, and bring to a rapid boil. Reduce the heat and simmer for about 30 minutes. Add the uncooked buckwheat.

2. Clean the button mushrooms (I suggest gently wiping them with a damp cloth or kitchen paper instead of washing them) and cut them into quarters. Mince the remaining onion and grate the remaining carrot using a box grater. Heat a little sunflower oil in a saucepan over medium heat, add the vegetables and the quartered mushrooms, and sauté everything until tender and fragrant.

3. Chop the wild mushrooms into medium pieces and add them to a small saucepan. Cover with cold water and bring to a boil. Drain the water and cover with cold water a second time. Bring to a boil once more and simmer over low heat until the mushrooms are tender. Drain and add the mushrooms to the vegetable broth.

4. Peel and dice the potatoes and add them to the broth. Cook until the potatoes are tender. Then add the sautéed vegetables, bay leaf, and allspice, simmer for a few minutes, and remove from the heat. Salt to taste and serve.

2 medium carrots
2 large onions
¼ stalk celery
½ cup (70 grams) uncooked
    buckwheat groats
1 pound (450 grams) button
    mushrooms
2 tablespoons sunflower oil
½ pound (200 grams) fresh porcini
    or other edible
    wild mushrooms
3 to 4 medium potatoes
1 bay leaf
2 allspice berries
Coarse salt to taste

cold borsch with greens

Холодний борщ із зеленню

serves 4

start to finish:
*1 hour
25 minutes*

4 large beetroots, scrubbed
1 bunch sorrel or spinach
4 cups (1 litre) Rye Bread
  Kvas (page 243) or
  Beetroot Kvas (page 244)
Coarse salt and freshly ground
  black pepper to taste
2 potatoes, unpeeled and boiled
Honey mustard for serving

While traveling across Ukraine, I stumbled across a fascinating recipe for green borsch, a popular spring dish that, despite its name, doesn't usually contain beetroots. However, this recipe, unlike traditional green borsch, called for beetroot kvas—which gave it a vibrant red hue—and lots of fresh herbs. I played around with the ingredients a little, replacing the beetroot kvas with dark kvas and the juice of cooked beetroots, but I made sure the bright red colour and the intense fresh flavour stayed the same. This is the perfect dish for a hot summer's day—it's refreshing, full of nutrients, and will keep you sated when you don't feel like cooking something more substantial.

1. Peel 2 of the beetroots, roughly dice them, and set them aside. Bake or boil the remaining 2 beetroots, unpeeled, until tender enough to be pierced with a fork. Wash and finely mince the sorrel or spinach and any other greens you're using.

2. Using a juicer or a food processor with a juicing attachment, juice the raw beetroots. Combine their juice with the dark kvas. The ratio should be approximately 1 to 1, but the amount of juice you'll get will depend on the size and variety of the beetroots. Add a little salt to taste and set aside.

3. Peel the 2 baked or boiled beetroots and cut them into medium cubes. Peel the 2 potatoes and cut them into cubes of roughly the same size. Combine the beetroots and the potatoes in a large mixing bowl. Add the chopped greens and season to taste.

4. Add ½ to 1 teaspoon of honey mustard to every serving dish. Top with the potatoes, cubed beetroots, and greens. Pour the beetroot juice mixture over the rest of the ingredients. Serve the soup cold.

The Authentic Ukrainian Kitchen

Main
Dishes

zrazy with mushrooms

serves 6 to 8 | start to finish: *1 hour*

pictured on pages 134–135

Зрази з грибами

Once potatoes became an integral part of Ukrainian cuisine, the various regions of the country developed their own potato-based dishes. Potato patties—zrazy—were typical of the Polissia region. For everyday meals, zrazy were filled with mushrooms, fish, or onions, while for holidays, they were stuffed with beef or pork.

Traditionally, the dough for zrazy was kneaded into a uniform mass with the vegetables or meat; it wasn't until later that variations with fillings appeared. This type of zrazy is the most common today.

Zrazy are fried in a skillet with sunflower oil or lard, but I opted for a healthier version by baking them in the oven; they turn out just as delicious. For the filling, I chose regular button mushrooms that can be bought anywhere.

Zrazy can be enjoyed on their own or with soured cream, adjika tomato sauce, or ketchup.

for the zrazy

6 medium potatoes
2 garlic cloves, peeled and crushed
1½ cups (120 grams) button mushrooms
1 large onion
½ ounce (15 grams) unsalted butter
3 egg yolks
Coarse salt and freshly ground black pepper to taste
7 ounces (200 grams) plain flour

1. Preheat the oven to 190°C/375°F/Gas 5 and line a baking sheet with baking paper. Set aside.

2. Peel the potatoes, cut them into medium cubes, and place in a large saucepan. Add the crushed garlic cloves, cover with cold water, and bring to a rapid boil over medium heat. Reduce the heat and cook the potatoes until tender, then drain, mash until no large lumps remain, and set aside to cool completely.

3. While the potatoes are cooling, wipe the mushrooms down with moist kitchen paper to get rid of any dirt, and finely mince them. Peel and finely mince the onion. Heat the butter until sizzling in a large frying pan over medium heat and add the minced mushrooms. Sauté them for a minute or two, then add the minced onion. Cook everything until tender and fragrant and transfer to a paper-towel-lined plate to get rid of the remaining moisture.

4. Once the mashed potatoes are cool, whisk in 2 of the egg yolks and add a little salt and freshly ground black pepper. Stir in the flour and mix well to combine.

5. Assemble the zrazy: Wet your hands with a little cold water to prevent the mixture from sticking. Scoop up a heaped tablespoon of the potato mixture, roll it into a ball, then flatten it into a disk. Place about a teaspoon of the mushroom mixture into the centre of the potato disk and cover it with a little more of the potato mixture. Carefully shape the mushroom-filled patty into an oval, making sure that the filling is completely sealed inside. Place the filled zrazy onto the lined baking sheet and repeat the process until you have used up all the potato mixture and all the filling.

6. Brush the zrazy with the remaining egg yolk and bake them in the preheated oven for about 20 minutes.

7. To make the khmeli suneli spice mix, combine all the ingredients in a spice or coffee grinder and grind everything to a fine powder. Store in an airtight container.

8. While the patties are baking, make the tomato sauce: wash the tomatoes and the red peppers and cut them into large chunks, discarding the seeds and membranes. Crush and peel the garlic cloves and remove the seeds from the chilli pepper. Transfer everything to a blender or food processor and blitz until chunky but well combined. Season with the salt, sugar, and spice mix and add the vinegar. Stir with a wooden or silicone spoon until everything is well combined.

9. Serve the prepared zrazy with adjika, soured cream, or ketchup. Zrazy are delightful whether served warm or cold.

for the khmeli suneli spice mix

2 teaspoons fenugreek seeds
1 teaspoon chilli powder
2 teaspoons dried parsley
2 teaspoons dried marjoram
1 teaspoon ground coriander
2 teaspoons dried dill
1 teaspoon ground black pepper
2 teaspoons coarse salt

for the adjika tomato sauce

1 pound (450 grams) tomatoes
1 pound (450 grams) red
    peppers
6 to 7 garlic cloves, to taste
Whole red chilli
2 teaspoons coarse salt
1 teaspoon granulated sugar
1 teaspoon khmeli suneli spice mix
    (this can be found in Eastern
    European grocery stores or
    online, but you can also make it
    at home; see above)
2 tablespoons white wine vinegar

halushky with sour cherries

Галушки з вишнями

Halushky are iconic dumplings that hail from the Poltava region. In the past, they were eaten almost every day because they are quite simple to make: Pieces of dough are cooked in boiling water, then served with sautéed onions and cracklings. There are different versions of halushky. When small pieces are pinched off the prepared dough and dropped into boiling water, as in this recipe, they are called pinched halushky. When the dough is rolled out and then cut into pieces with a knife, they're called cut halushky.

Halushky are usually savoury, but in this version, I decided to combine the savoury dough with slightly sweet cherries. It is incredibly delicious!

There is also a version of stuffed halushky that is steamed with different fillings. You can find the recipe for Steamed Halushky on page 139.

1. Bring a large saucepan of salted water to a boil over medium heat. Meanwhile, prepare the dough. In a large mixing bowl, combine the flour, kefir, egg, and salt. Knead the dough until it is soft and tacky but not too sticky.

2. Once the water is boiling, pinch off small pieces of dough and toss them into the saucepan. Cook the halushky for 2 minutes or until they start floating up to the surface, then fish them out with a slotted spoon. Drizzle the cooked halushky with oil so they won't stick together. Cover with a tea towel and leave in a warm place to ensure that they don't cool before serving.

3. Prepare the cherry sauce: Place a medium pan on medium heat and add the defrosted and pitted cherries along with their juices. Stir in the cinnamon and sugar and cook for a few minutes or until the sugar dissolves completely and the mixture thickens enough to coat the back of a spoon.

4. Place the halushky in a large serving bowl and ladle the cherry sauce over them. Serve hot with soured cream.

serves 4 to 6 | start to finish: *45 minutes*

for the halushky

3½ cups (450 grams) plain flour
1 cup (250 millilitres) kefir, buttermilk, or thin natural yogurt
1 large egg
½ teaspoon coarse salt

for the cherry sauce

1 pound (450 grams) frozen sour cherries, defrosted and pitted
½ teaspoon ground cinnamon
½ cup (100 grams) sugar

to serve

½ cup (125 millilitres) soured cream

steamed halushky

Парові галушки з курячою печінкою

serves 4 to 6 | start to finish: *1 hour*

Another way to make traditional Ukrainian halushky is by stuffing the pieces of dough with various types of filling and steaming them. My favourite stuffing for this dish is a rich, creamy filling made from chicken livers.

Traditionally, stuffed halushky were popular all across the left bank of Ukraine (a historic region stretching eastward from the Dnipro River). They were cooked with offal, meat, or boiled tongue and sometimes with the addition of fried or dried vegetables.

1. Make the dough for the dumplings: in a large mixing bowl, whisk together the flour, bicarbonate of soda, and salt and slowly drizzle in the kefir. Mix everything until well combined. Using your hands, knead the dough until it is smooth and elastic. Shape it into a ball, transfer it to a lightly floured surface, cover with a kitchen towel, and let rest for about 20 minutes.

2. While the dough is resting, make the filling: Clean and trim the chicken livers, removing any visible veins and silverskin. Add the livers to a small saucepan, cover with cold water, and bring to a boil over medium heat. Reduce the heat, add a generous pinch of salt and pepper, and cook the livers at a gentle simmer for about 15 minutes. Finely mince the onion and sauté it in the sunflower oil over medium heat until golden and fragrant. Mince the garlic cloves and add them to the frying pan, sauté everything for a few minutes more, then remove the pan from the heat. Once the chicken livers are cooked through, drain them and run them through a meat grinder or pulse in a food processor until creamy. In a mixing bowl, combine the minced chicken livers with the fried onion mixture. Let cool completely.

3. Divide the dough into two halves. Place one of the halves back under the towel and divide the second into 12 equal pieces. Roll each one out into a small flat disk, spoon about a teaspoon of the filling into the centre, and seal it shut. Place the filled dumplings seam-side down onto a baking sheet lined with baking paper and repeat the process with the second half of the dough. You should end up with about 24 small dumplings.

4. Heat a large steamer over medium-high heat. Steam the dumplings for about 15 minutes or until glossy and puffed up (you'll need to do this in batches). Brush the cooked buns generously with the melted butter and serve warm.

for the dough

4 cups (540 grams) plain flour
½ teaspoon bicarbonate of soda
Pinch of coarse salt
1⅓ cups (330 millilitres) kefir, buttermilk, or thin natural yogurt

for the filling

14 ounces (400 grams) chicken livers
Coarse salt and freshly ground black pepper
1 large onion
2 tablespoons sunflower oil
2 garlic cloves
6¼ ounces (180 grams) unsalted butter, melted

deruny

potato pancakes   *Деруни*

Deruny—small pancakes made of grated potatoes—are beloved all over Ukraine. In some regions, they are called tertyukhy (which means "grated pancakes"). If you want to experience a real deruny extravaganza, visit Korosten during the annual potato-pancake festival; thousands of deruny lovers flock there to enjoy their favourite potato dish.

Of course there are arguments about the best way to make deruny. Some prefer grating the potatoes on a Microplane to get a smooth, pancake-like texture, while others say that roughly grated potatoes are the only way to go. I side with the latter group, since there's nothing better than deruny with crispy, crunchy golden edges!

1. Preheat the oven to 200°C/400°F/Gas 6. Line a baking sheet with baking paper (This step is optional but recommended; baking the deruny for a few minutes after frying will make them more tender on the inside.)

2. Using a box grater, grate a little bit of the peeled onion into a medium bowl. Grate some of the potatoes into the same bowl, then switch back to grating the onion. (Alternating between the onion and the potatoes will prevent the mixture from browning.)

3. Place a sieve or a strainer over a large bowl, transfer the grated onion and potatoes into it, and gently squeeze the excess liquid out. Transfer the mixture into a dry bowl, add a generous pinch of salt, and stir in the egg. Add a little freshly ground black pepper and, if desired, grate the clove of garlic using a Microplane. Add it to the mixture. Mix everything well to combine.

4. Heat the oil in a large nonstick pan over medium heat. With a tablespoon, scoop up portions of the potato mixture and carefully place them in the hot oil. Use the spoon to tidy up the edges of the deruny and flatten them out a little. Try to keep them from touching one another. Fry them for 3 to 4 minutes per side, until golden and crispy around the edges.

5. Optional: transfer the cooked deruny to the lined baking sheet and set them aside while you fry the rest of the deruny. Once all the deruny have been fried, bake them in the preheated oven for 5 to 10 minutes. Serve warm, with soured cream on the side.

1 small onion, peeled
5 medium waxy potatoes, peeled
Coarse salt and freshly ground pepper
1 large egg
1 clove garlic (optional)
5 tablespoons sunflower oil (or other neutral oil)
3 tablespoons soured cream for serving (optional)

knish

makes
2 large pies

start to finish:
1 hour
20 minutes

puff pastry pie with cheese and potato filling　　　*Книш*

If you search the internet for information about the pastry called knish, you will probably come across recipes from Ashkenazi Jewish cuisine. The knish is somewhat similar to small enclosed pies, baked or deep-fried. The filling can vary; traditionally, it's just boiled potatoes, but some versions use grains, cheese, or even meat.

I was surprised to learn that knish is also considered traditional in Boiko cuisine. The Boikos, one of the largest ethnic groups in the Carpathian Highlands, have unique culinary traditions. Boiko-style knish is made with yeast dough and filled with mashed potatoes, fried onions, and cracklings.

In this version, I throw in some nuts and cheese to give the pastry an even more vibrant flavour.

5 large potatoes, peeled
Coarse salt
1 large onion
3 tablespoons sunflower oil
⅓ cup (100 grams) walnuts
Freshly ground black pepper
1 cup (10 grams) grated firm goat's
　　cheese
2 pounds (1 kilogram) frozen puff
　　pastry, thawed until pliable
Plain flour, for dusting
1 large egg yolk
1 bunch parsley

1. Dice the potatoes, add them to a small saucepan, cover with cold water, add a generous pinch of salt, and bring to a boil over medium heat. Reduce the heat and cook the potatoes at a steady simmer for about 20 minutes or until they are tender and easily pierced with a fork.

2. While the potatoes are cooking, peel the onion, finely mince it, and sauté it in a little oil until golden and fragrant. Finely chop the walnuts and set them aside.

3. Once the potatoes are done, drain them and mash into a smooth paste. Season to taste with salt and freshly ground black pepper. Stir in the chopped walnuts, sautéed onion, and grated goat's cheese.

4. Assemble the knishes: Line a large baking sheet with baking paper and preheat the oven to 190°C/375°F/Gas 5. Split the puff pastry in half and place one half under a sheet of plastic wrap or a towel. On a lightly floured surface, roll the other half of the pastry into a large rectangle. Place a generous portion of the filling in the centre of the rectangle and fold the corners of the pastry up to partially cover the filling. Tuck the ends in and pinch the seams together so that the filling doesn't seep out during baking. Transfer the knish to the lined baking sheet and repeat the process with the second half of the dough and the remainder of the filling. Brush the knishes with the egg yolk and bake in the preheated oven for about 40 minutes. Garnish the baked knishes with fresh parsley leaves.

courgette fritters

serves 4 to 6 | start to finish: *25 minutes*

Оладки з кабачків

Ukrainians are fond of all sorts of pancakes, and they are especially popular in summer, when markets and grocery stores are flooded with freshly harvested courgette and other seasonal produce. It might sound like an odd addition to pancake batter, but trust me—a little grated courgette works wonders to make the pancakes even more tender and delicate. Of course, nowadays you can buy courgette at any time of the year, so there's no need to wait to try out this recipe!

1. Wash the courgette and pat it dry. Using the coarse side of a box grater, grate it into a medium bowl. Add salt and pepper to taste. Mix in the egg. Wash the parsley well, finely mince it, and add it to the courgette mixture.

2. Stir in the soured cream, add the flour, and mix everything well to combine. The mixture should resemble a sticky, thick pancake batter.

3. Add the oil to a medium frying pan placed over medium heat. Once the oil starts sizzling, drop several heaped tablespoons of the mixture into it, making sure not to overcrowd the pan. Fry the fritters for about 2 minutes per side.

4. Place the cooked fritters on a large kitchen-paper-lined plate. Keep frying the fritters until you use up all the batter.

5. Prepare the sauce: finely mince the mint leaves and, in a small bowl, combine them with the yogurt. Season to taste with salt and pepper and add the finely minced clove of garlic. Stir well and serve alongside the warm courgette pancakes.

for the fritters

1 medium courgette
Coarse salt and freshly ground
    black pepper to taste
1 large egg
5 sprigs parsley
2 tablespoons soured cream
4 to 5 tablespoons (30 to
    45 grams) plain flour, as needed
5 tablespoons vegetable oil

for the yogurt sauce

5 sprigs mint
1 cup (250 grams) natural yogurt
Coarse salt and freshly ground
    black pepper to taste
1 clove garlic, finely minced

fish in soured cream sauce

serves 4 to 6 | start to finish: 45 minutes

Короп в сметані

Carp or other freshwater fish baked in a rich soured cream-based sauce are a traditional fisherman's favourite. Historically, the freshly caught fish would be placed whole in a ceramic dish, covered in a generous layer of sauce, and baked in a wood-fired oven until the fish became incredibly tender. Nowadays we can get the same flavour by simply baking the fish in an ordinary kitchen oven, and you can get fresh fish from the nearest supermarket; you don't have to sit by a cold river all day.

This sauce works perfectly for both whole fish and fish fillets. It is also a great match for ocean fish, such as hake, pollock, and perch.

1 whole leek
5 tablespoons sunflower oil, as needed
5 sprigs dill
2 garlic cloves
2 whole carp (or other medium freshwater fish), each about 1 pound (450 grams), gutted and cleaned, fins trimmed, heads and tails still on
Coarse salt and freshly ground black pepper
5 tablespoons plain flour
2 cups (500 millilitres) soured cream
1 cup (250 millilitres) double cream

1. Cut the leek into thin slices and set it aside. Brush a large baking dish with a teaspoon of the sunflower oil and set it aside. Finely mince the dill and the garlic and also set them aside.

2. Pat the fish dry with kitchen paper and season them well with salt and pepper on the outside and inside the cavities. At this point I suggest letting the fish rest in the refrigerator for up to an hour; this helps them become really flavourful.

3. Preheat the oven to 190°C/375°F/Gas 5.

4. Remove the fish from the refrigerator, let them come to room temperature for 10 to 15 minutes, then roll them in a generous amount of flour. Heat the remaining oil in a large skillet over medium heat. Once the oil starts shimmering, gently place the carp in the pan and sear them well on both sides, moving the fish as little as possible. Once the fish are crisp and golden on both sides, remove the pan from the heat.

5. Arrange half of the leek slices on the bottom of the baking dish and place the fried fish on top. In a medium bowl, whisk together the soured cream and the cream. Season the mixture to taste and pour it over and around the carp. Sprinkle the remaining leeks and the minced dill and garlic on top of the fish and place the baking dish in the preheated oven. Bake for 20 to 30 minutes. Serve hot.

boiled potatoes with salted herring

serves 2 to 4 | **start to finish:**
*30 minutes,
plus 1 hour for
soaking herring*

Відварна картопля з солоним оселедцем

Potatoes and herring aren't a uniquely Ukrainian dish; similar dishes can be found in German and Danish cuisines, among others. But this humble dish is so popular in Ukraine that I must mention it. And I've got a trick to make it even better: Before you start cooking, soak the herring in milk—it will make it a little less salty and more tender!

If you can't find salted herring, use marinated herring. There is no need to soak the herring in milk if you use the marinated fish.

1. Debone and fillet the herring: using a sharp paring knife, cut the head off right below the fins. Remove the insides and the skin from both sides of the fish, cut the tail off, and carefully detach the herring fillets from the bones.

2. In a large bowl, put the herring fillets in the milk. Place the bowl in the refrigerator for an hour—this will make the fish taste a little less salty and bitter, and it will make the texture a lot more tender.

3. Wash and peel the potatoes, roughly dice them, and set aside (if using young potatoes, you can just scrub them and boil them whole and unpeeled). Place the potatoes in a large saucepan, add enough cold water to fully submerge them, and bring to a rapid boil over medium-high heat. Reduce heat to a simmer, cover, and cook for about 20 minutes or until the potatoes can easily be pierced with a fork. While the potatoes are cooking, finely mince the dill. Peel the onion, cut it in half, and thinly slice both halves. Set the sliced onions and the minced dill aside.

4. Once the potatoes have cooked through, drain them and add the butter and the minced dill. Toss everything well to combine. Drain, dry, and slice the herring fillets. Serve the potatoes alongside the finely sliced onions and the herring fillets.

1 whole salted herring
1 cup plus 2 tablespoons
   (275 millilitres) whole milk
5 large potatoes
3 sprigs dill
1 large red onion
2½ ounces (45 grams) unsalted
   butter

banosh

Банош

This traditional Hutsul corn porridge hails all the way from the Carpathian Mountains. If you want to explore the amazing variety of flavours from all over Ukraine, you'll definitely have to try this one out—right after borsch, that is. There are countless ways to make banosh, and arguing as to which one is the "real" one is pointless. Of course, authentic Hutsul banosh should be cooked in a cauldron over an open fire to capture that smoky aroma, so I'm just going to share my version of the recipe. It's one of the best ones I've ever tried.

5 ounces (140 grams) salo or fatty bacon, cubed
2 cups (500 millilitres) whole milk
1 cup (160 grams) polenta
½ ounce (15 grams) unsalted butter
1 tablespoon soured cream
½ cup (60 grams) crumbled goat's cheese
Coarse salt and freshly ground black pepper to taste

1. Add the cubed salo or bacon to a small frying pan. Place it over medium heat and fry until most of the fat has rendered and the salo or bacon pieces are golden brown and crispy.

2. Meanwhile, add the milk to a medium saucepan. Bring it to a boil over medium heat and add the polenta. Reduce heat to a simmer, mix well to combine, and cook, stirring occasionally, for about 15 minutes or until the mixture thickens to a slurry with distinct granules. Stir in the butter and the soured cream. Season to taste.

3. Take the saucepan off the heat and transfer the polenta to a large, deep bowl. Garnish with the fried salo or bacon cubes and the crumbled goat's cheese. Season to taste with salt and pepper. Serve hot!

pearl barley with mushrooms

Перлова крупа з грибами

serves 4

start to finish:
*30 minutes,
plus 1 to 3 hours
for soaking*

Pearl barley is not widely mentioned in the history of Ukrainian cuisine, although some cooked it as porridge; others added it to sausage fillings. Even in modern Ukrainian cuisine, pearl barley is far less popular than grains like buckwheat, rice, and millet. But I want to shift this trend and incorporate more pearl barley into the diet of Ukrainians because it is tasty, affordable, and healthy. Try cooking pearl barley with vegetables and button mushrooms, oyster mushrooms, or any type of wild mushrooms; you'll love it.

1½ cups (280 grams) pearl barley
2 cups (500 millilitres) cold water
4 cups (270 grams) button mushrooms
1 large onion
2 tablespoons sunflower oil
¾ ounce (20 grams) unsalted butter
Coarse salt and freshly ground black pepper
Fresh parsley for garnishing

1. Soak the pearl barley in a bowl of cold water for 1 to 3 hours. Drain the water, rinse the barley, and transfer it to a medium saucepan. Cover with fresh cold water and bring to a boil over medium heat. Reduce the heat, cover, and cook at a gentle simmer for about 25 minutes. The barley is done when it has tripled in volume, absorbed most of the water, and is soft yet chewy. Make sure you do not overcook it, as you don't want it to become mushy.

2. Carefully clean the mushrooms with a damp cloth, trimming the ends of the stalks with a sharp knife if necessary. Quarter the mushrooms and set aside. Peel the onion and finely mince it. Heat the sunflower oil in a large pan and fry the quartered mushrooms until golden on all sides, working in batches to avoid overcrowding the pan. Once all the mushrooms are nice and golden, add the minced onion to the pan and sauté until golden and fragrant. Season to taste with salt and freshly ground black pepper.

3. Divide the cooked pearl barley among several deep bowls, add a little butter to each bowl, and top with the cooked mushrooms and onions. Garnish with a little fresh parsley and serve warm.

millet kulish
with bacon

Пшоняний куліш з беконом

Historians believe that the first recipes for kulish, also known as "field porridge," date back to the Cossack days. Cossacks would combine millet with lard-fried onions and cook the mixture in a large cauldron on an open hearth. It was convenient (what better way is there to make porridge for a whole army?) and delicious, especially when garnished with herbs and a little crumbly cheese.

Well-prepared kulish features fully cooked millet and a uniform texture. It is worth noting that authentic Cossack kulish, prepared in field conditions, was made solely from millet fried in oil with garlic and seasoned with salt. As time went on, peasants began to add salo, meat, cheese, and even fish to the kulish, resulting in a wide range of variations. I recommend trying some of these versions for a unique culinary experience.

Now you can re-create this legendary dish in your own kitchen.

4 ounces (115 grams) salo or
   thick-cut bacon
1 large onion, peeled
2 to 3 garlic cloves, to taste
¼ celeriac, peeled
1 medium carrot, peeled
1 parsley root, peeled
3 tablespoons vegetable oil
2 cups (500 millilitres) whole milk
3½ cups (800 millilitres) water
2 bay leaves
5 allspice berries
3 medium potatoes, peeled
1 cup (185 grams) millet
Coarse salt and freshly ground
   black pepper to taste
1 ounce (30 grams) Carpathian
   bryndza cheese (or other
   sheep's-milk cheese, such
   as feta)
Parsley and dill for garnishing

1. Roughly cut the salo or bacon into cubes. In a medium frying pan over medium heat, fry the cubes until most of the fat has rendered and they turn golden brown.

2. Dice the onion. Using the flat side of a large chef's knife, crush the garlic cloves and mince them. Add the onion and the garlic to the pan and sauté in the rendered bacon fat until fragrant and translucent.

3. Dice the celeriac, carrot, and parsley root and add them to the pan along with the vegetable oil. After sautéing everything for a few minutes, add the milk and water to the pan. Reduce heat to a low simmer and let everything cook for about 10 minutes. Add the bay leaves and allspice.

4. Dice the potatoes and add them to the pan.

5. While the potatoes and vegetables are cooking, add the millet to a large bowl and cover with hot water. Once the water cools enough to handle, rinse and drain the millet well. This will help rid the millet of the bitter aftertaste it sometimes has.

6. Add the rinsed millet to the pan, mix everything well to combine, and cook over low heat for about 30 minutes or until the vegetables and potatoes are tender and the millet has cooked through and thickened to a porridge-like texture. Let cook a little longer and add salt and freshly ground black pepper to taste.

7. Before serving, garnish with crumbled bryndza (or other sheep's-milk cheese of your choice) and a few sprigs of parsley and dill. Serve hot!

homemade kovbasa with garlic

serves 4 to 6 | start to finish: *1 hour 40 minutes*

Домашня ковбаса з часником

When you see this recipe for kovbasa—Ukrainian sausage—you might think, *Yevhen, have you lost your mind? Making sausage is an incredibly difficult, long, and messy process—why would I go to all that hassle when I can get perfectly good sausages from my butcher or the nearest supermarket?*

I get it—the very idea of making sausages at home can be intimidating, especially if you don't have all that much free time or you are a novice home cook. But trust me, the process isn't half as complicated as it seems, and the result is so good, you won't regret spending an evening in the kitchen.

So if you're wondering if you should give this recipe a try, let me tell you that for Ukrainian people, making sausages is no more complicated than frying potatoes. You might be surprised at how easy it is.

1 teaspoon bicarbonate of soda

10 feet (3 metres) natural sausage casings

4½ pounds (2 kilograms) lean pork shoulder

3 heads garlic

1 tablespoon coarse salt

1 tablespoon freshly ground black pepper

1 cup (250 millilitres) ice-cold water

special equipment: meat grinder (or meat-grinder attachment for a stand mixer) and sausage-stuffing attachment

1. In a large bowl, combine several cups of warm water with the bicarbonate of soda. Soak the sausage casings for a few minutes to get rid of the excess salt and rinse them with cool water. Soaking the sausage casings will also make them easier to attach to the stuffer attachment. You can get artificial sausage casings instead, but I prefer the natural hog casing (you can get intestines from a reputable butcher or at a farmers' market).

2. Cut the pork shoulder into cubes small enough to fit into your meat grinder. Separate the garlic cloves, and crush, peel, and finely mince about a third of them. Set aside. Using a meat grinder, grind the meat and the remaining garlic and transfer the mixture into a large bowl.

3. Season the ground meat with salt, freshly ground pepper, and minced garlic. Carefully mix the ingredients with a wooden spoon for 10 to 15 minutes until the sausage mixture becomes denser and resembles a sticky paste (you can also do this using a stand mixer equipped with a paddle attachment). Slowly drizzle in the ice-cold water and mix thoroughly until the meat absorbs all the liquid.

4. Cut the casings into 15- to 25-inch (38- to 61-centimetre) segments and fill them with the sausage blend using a sausage stuffer. Make sure you
fill the casings as tightly as possible. Close the ends with kitchen twine or just knot them tightly and trim the ends. If you like, you can freeze the uncooked sausages at this point for up to three months.

5. Preheat the oven to 190°C/375°F/Gas 5. Arrange the stuffed sausages on a baking-paper-lined baking sheet, and, using a cocktail stick or a sharp paring knife, make a few small holes in the casings—this will keep the sausages from exploding as the meat filling expands during the cooking. Roast for about 50 minutes or until the surface of the sausages turns dark and crispy.

krovianka

blood sausage   *Кров'янка*

Back in the day, Ukrainian families in villages and small towns made their own sausages out of pig's blood mixed with buckwheat. It was a good way to reduce waste after butchering a pig, and despite how it sounds, pig's-blood sausage is delicious. After a while, krovianka (blood sausages) became popular in large cities all over Ukraine. Now it is made by professional butchers or farmers and can be found in most supermarkets, but I still believe that homemade is best, even if the recipe requires a little patience.

1. Preheat the oven to 190°C/375°F/Gas 5.

2. Put the pork belly through the meat grinder (I suggest cooling the pork in the fridge or freezer beforehand, as this will make the grinding much easier), then transfer the ground meat to a large mixing bowl.

3. If using unstrained pig's blood, strain it through a sieve to remove any clots. Set the filtered blood aside, put the blood clots through the meat grinder, and add them to the ground pork belly.

4. Add the cooked buckwheat, salt and pepper generously, add the ground cardamom and minced garlic, and mix well to combine, slowly drizzling in the milk. Stir in the blood and mix everything until well combined.

5. Fill a large bowl with warm water and stir in the teaspoon of bicarbonate of soda. Soak the sausage casings for a few minutes to get rid of the excess salt and then rinse them in cold water. Soaking the sausage casings will make them easier to attach to the stuffer attachment. You can get artificial sausage casings, but I prefer the natural hog casing (you can get intestines from a reputable butcher or at the farmers' market).

6. Cut the casings into 15- to 25-inch (38- to 61-centimetre) segments and fill them with the blood-sausage blend using a sausage stuffer. Make sure you fill the casing as tightly as possible. Close the ends with kitchen twine or just knot them tightly and trim the ends. If you like, you can freeze the uncooked sausage at this point for up to three months.

7. Bring a large saucepan of salted water to a boil. Once the water is at a steady boil, reduce the heat and cook the stuffed sausages for 10 to 15 minutes. Drain them and arrange the sausages in a large baking dish lightly brushed down with oil. Using a cocktail stick or a sharp paring knife, make a few small holes in the casings; this will keep the sausages from exploding as the meat filling expands during cooking.

8. Roast for about 30 minutes, occasionally brushing the sausage with the pan juices.

10 ounces (280 grams) pork belly, trimmed and cut into ⅛- to ¼-inch (3- to 5-millimetre) cubes

6 cups (1.5 litres) fresh pig's blood, preferably unstrained

2 cups (250 grams) cooked buckwheat (preferably a day old)

Coarse salt and freshly ground black pepper to taste

A few pinches of ground cardamom

10 garlic cloves, minced

1 cup (250 millilitres) whole milk

1 teaspoon bicarbonate of soda

12 feet (4 metres) natural sausage casings

special equipment: meat grinder (or meat-grinder attachment) and sausage-stuffing attachment for a stand mixer

kruchenyky

mushroom-stuffed pork rolls   *Кручеными*

Old Ukrainian cookbooks often mention kruchenyky, sometimes referred to as zavyvanyky—delicate pork rolls stuffed with various fillings. A piece of pork or beef was pounded thin, filled, and rolled up into a roulade. They could be small or large, depending on what the homemaker fancied. Like most meat dishes, kruchenyky were traditionally prepared for holidays and served alongside boiled potatoes or porridge.

You might come across variations with smoked prunes or vegetables, but I'm a fan of kruchenyky stuffed with mushrooms. You can make them with any kind of mushrooms—ordinary button mushrooms, oyster mushrooms, wild mushrooms, or a mix of them all.

1. Line a cutting board with plastic wrap, place the cutlets in a single layer on the cutting board, and cover with another layer of plastic wrap. Thoroughly pound the cutlets with a meat mallet until ¼ to ⅛ inch (5 to 3 millimetres) thick. Be careful while pounding the meat; it will tear if you're too rough or if it gets too thin. Sprinkle a little salt and pepper onto the pounded cutlets and set aside.

2. Wipe the mushrooms down with a moist kitchen paper and trim off the dirty bits of the mushroom stalks. Quarter them and set aside. Peel the onion and dice it. Heat the sunflower oil in a medium pan over medium heat and sauté the mushrooms until golden brown. In a separate pan, sauté the diced onions in a little sunflower oil over medium heat until translucent and fragrant. Combine the mushrooms and onions in a small bowl.

3. Place about 2 tablespoons of the filling in the centre of each cutlet, carefully roll it into an envelope-like shape, and tuck in the edges. Instead of fastening them with cocktail sticks or butcher's twine, pound one of the edges even thinner and then roll it over the rest of the roulade. Using your hands, carefully shape the rolls into ovals.

4. Heat a little oil in a large pan over medium heat and sear the meat rolls until golden brown and crispy on all sides.

5. Make the sauce: Preheat the oven to 190°C/375°F/Gas 5. Using a box grater, grate the peeled carrot and set it aside. Peel and dice the onion. Heat the sunflower oil in a medium pan over medium heat, add the carrot and the onion, and sauté until the onion is fragrant and translucent. Stir in the tomato purée and deglaze with ½ cup (120 millilitres) water. Stir well and sauté the vegetables until most of the liquid has evaporated. Salt and pepper to taste.

6. Place the meat rolls in a lightly oiled ovenproof dish and cover with the sauce. Bake in the preheated oven for 20 minutes.

---

makes about 6 rolls | **start to finish: *50 minutes***

1 pound (450 grams) lean pork, trimmed and cut into 6 equal cutlets
Coarse salt and freshly ground black pepper to taste
1 pound (450 grams) button mushrooms
1 large onion
3 tablespoons sunflower oil

for the sauce

1 large carrot, peeled
1 large onion
2 tablespoons sunflower oil
2 tablespoons tomato purée
Coarse salt and pepper to taste

lazy holubtsi

serves 6 to 8 | start to finish: *1 hour 30 minutes*

stuffed cabbage rolls   *Ліниві голубці*

Holubtsi—stuffed cabbage rolls—are very popular in all regions of Ukraine. Naturally, the people in each region have their own unique way of cooking them and use slightly different ingredients. Some make holubtsi stuffed with millet, others with buckwheat, but in most versions nowadays, rice is used, even though it's not traditionally Ukrainian. The original recipe involves carefully separating a head of cabbage into leaves—you remove the core and slightly blanch the cabbage in boiling water to soften the leaves and make the process easier. The cabbage leaves are then stuffed with ground meat mixed with grains, and the stuffed parcels are simmered in sauce.

However, inventive Ukrainians found a way to capture the taste of holubtsi without investing so much time. This is how the recipe for lazy holubtsi appeared, and it has become quite popular. It's this recipe that I'd like to share with you.

¾ cup (130 grams) medium-grain white rice such as Arborio
1 large onion
1 large carrot, peeled
½ small head white cabbage, cored
2 tablespoons sunflower oil
1½ ounces (40 grams) unsalted butter
Coarse salt and freshly ground black pepper
1¼ pounds (550 grams) minced beef
½ teaspoon ground coriander
One 14-ounce (400-gram) can peeled, chopped tomatoes
1 cup (250 millilitres) soured cream

1. Preheat the oven to 190°C/375°F/Gas 5.

2. Thoroughly rinse the rice in cold water until it runs clear. Transfer the rice to a large saucepan and add 1 cup (250 millilitres) cold salted water. Bring the rice to a boil over medium heat and cook, covered, for about 5 minutes. Take the saucepan of the heat and let it rest, covered, for another 15 minutes. Let the rice cool completely.

3. Meanwhile, make the vegetable base: Peel and roughly dice the onion, grate the carrot, and thinly slice the cabbage. Heat the oil and butter in a large pan until foaming and add the chopped onions and sliced cabbage. Sauté them until the cabbage has softened but still has some snap and the onions are completely translucent. Then add the carrot and cook the vegetables for another 3 minutes, or until fragrant. Season to taste.

4. In a large mixing bowl, combine the cooked rice, ground meat, and cooked vegetables. Season with the coriander and mix everything until thoroughly combined. Using your hands, shape the mixture into small oval patties and arrange them in a large baking dish lightly greased with oil. It's all right if the patties touch—they will shrink a little while baking.

5. Make the sauce: whisk together the canned peeled tomatoes and soured cream. Drizzle the sauce generously over and around the patties.

6. Bake the lazy holubtsi in the preheated oven for 45 to 50 minutes.

shynka

traditional oven-baked ham

Шинка

serves 4 | start to finish: *3 hours*

This is probably the most popular and simplest way to prepare pork, and Ukrainians have been using it for centuries. The pork roast, sometimes called buzhenyna, is made in all regions of Ukraine, and the methods hardly vary. The most important thing is to generously stuff the meat with garlic. In Volyn and the Pre-Carpathians, pork for the roast was often soaked in a brine solution and then cooked in an oven slowly to make the meat tender. Workers placed slices of the roast on bread and took them to the harvest fields, as it was a filling and convenient snack. Today, pork roast is served with boiled or fried potatoes or porridge.

I suggest cooking the roast pork in baking paper, which will help the meat stay juicy. Keep in mind that if your piece of meat is large, it might require a bit more time to roast, around an hour and a half in the parchment packet.

2 tablespoons coarse salt
Freshly ground black pepper
1 pound (450 grams) boneless
   pork shoulder or loin
Cloves from 1½ garlic bulbs,
   peeled
1 tablespoon honey
1 tablespoon mild mustard

1. Generously salt and pepper the pork shoulder and massage the seasoning into all the crevices. Wrap the meat tightly in plastic wrap (this will help it retain the shape while baking) and let rest in the fridge for at least 1½ hours or preferably overnight.

2. Preheat the oven to 190°C/375°F/Gas 5. Remove the meat from the fridge and take off the plastic wrap. Dip each garlic clove in a little coarse salt. Make punctures all over the meat and insert the salt-dipped garlic cloves into the holes. Tightly wrap the garlic-studded meat in baking paper and transfer it to a baking dish. Bake in the preheated oven for about an hour.

3. While the meat is cooking, make the glaze: in a small bowl, mix the honey and mustard. After the meat has cooked for an hour, remove it from the oven and slice open the baking paper covering it. Generously brush the ham with the honey-mustard glaze and return it to the oven for about 20 more minutes or until it becomes golden brown.

4. Let cool completely before slicing. Serve cold.

beer-braised roast pork

serves 4 to 6 | start to finish: 2 hours 30 minutes

Свинина запечена з пивом

Traditionally, Ukrainians used kvas for cooking. In vereshchaka, for example, pieces of pork were braised in beetroot-based or bread-based kvas. Since finding kvas outside of Ukraine can be a little challenging (and making your own takes some time), I suggest replacing beetroot or bread kvas with beer. By the way, cooking meat in beer is quite popular in several European countries.

The flavour of meat cooked in beer rather than kvas will be slightly different—you won't get the distinct beetroot or bread flavour—but overall, it'll be similar to the traditional recipe. For this version, I recommend using only dark beer. The darker the beer, the better it'll taste.

1. Preheat the oven to 190°C/375°F/Gas 5.

2. Cut the pork shoulder into bite-size chunks, transfer to a large bowl, and season generously with salt and black pepper. Finely mince the garlic cloves and toss them with the meat chunks.

3. Heat the sunflower oil in a large frying pan over medium heat and sear the meat chunks until brown on all sides. Work in batches and do not overcrowd the pan or the meat might not get a good crust. Transfer the fried meat pieces to an ovenproof dish. Sprinkle the dried oregano over the meat and pour about three-quarters of the beer into the dish.

4. Place the meat in the preheated oven and bake for 1½ to 2 hours. While the meat is baking, make the sauce: deglaze the frying pan with the remaining beer and let most of the liquid cook off. Make a butter slurry (it will help thicken the sauce) by combining the softened butter and the flour until a dough-like substance forms and then stir it into the reduced beer mixture. Let the sauce cook for a few more minutes over low heat, stirring constantly, and set aside.

5. Let the baked meat cool a little. Divide it among several large plates, drizzle with a generous helping of the sauce, and sprinkle the breadcrumbs on top. Garnish each plate with a little fresh parsley and serve immediately.

2¼ pounds (1 kilogram) pork shoulder
Coarse salt and freshly ground black pepper to taste
1 small head garlic, cloves separated and peeled
3 tablespoons sunflower oil (or other neutral oil)
1 teaspoon dried oregano
3 cups (700 millilitres) dark beer or kvas
2½ ounces (45 grams) unsalted butter, softened to room temperature
2 tablespoons plain flour
1 tablespoon fresh breadcrumbs
3 sprigs parsley

kotleta po kyivsky

chicken Kyiv   *Котлета по-київськи*

serves 2 to 4   **start to finish:**
*2 hours
40 minutes,
possibly
overnight*

Unlike kulish and kruchenyky, chicken Kyiv isn't something you'll find recipes for in ancient culinary manuscripts. According to various sources, this dish appeared either at the end of the nineteenth century or the beginning of the twentieth century. There're so many versions of its origin that it's up to historians, not cooks, to research it. What is undeniable is that chicken Kyiv is one of the most iconic culinary symbols of the Ukrainian capital.

To make chicken Kyiv according to the original recipe, you need to dismantle a whole chicken in such a way that the breast fillet remains attached to the pelvic bone. The fillet has to be pounded, seasoned, stuffed with frozen butter mixed with chopped herbs, breaded, frozen, and then fried in a deep fryer. You'll agree that it isn't the easiest recipe to re-create at home.

That is why I'm going to give you a simplified version of this dish. It uses minced chicken and combines two cooking methods: deep-frying and oven-roasting. Trust me, the delicate flavour of these cutlets is just as exquisite as the original.

Just a heads-up—when you're cutting into a chicken Kyiv cutlet, be sure to do it carefully. If it was cooked properly and the butter didn't leak out, there's a chance it could splatter.

1 pound (450 grams) minced
  chicken
3 ounces (85 grams) bacon or salo,
  ground into a paste using a meat
  grinder or a food processor
Coarse salt and freshly ground
  black pepper to taste
1 small bunch dill
2⅛ ounces (60 grams) unsalted
  butter
2 large eggs
1 cup (130 grams) plain flour
1 cup (125 grams) dried
  breadcrumbs
Vegetable oil, for frying

1. In a mixing bowl, combine the minced chicken and the bacon. Add a generous pinch of salt and pepper and mix everything until a sticky paste forms. Set aside.

2. Finely mince the dill and set aside. Cut the butter into 6 slices and set aside.

3. Break the eggs into a medium bowl, mix well and set aside. Prepare two bowls, one with the flour and one with the breadcrumbs. Line a baking sheet with parchment.

4. Divide the meat mixture into 6 equal parts. Using your hands, roll one of the meat portions into an oval shape and press a slice of the butter and a teaspoon of the minced dill into the meat patty. Wrap the meat around the filling so that it is fully covered. Dredge the butter-filled patty in the flour, dip it in the egg wash, and coat well with the breadcrumbs. Place the breaded patty on the lined baking sheet and repeat the process with the remaining meat mixture.

recipe continues

5. Once all the meat patties have been filled with butter and breaded, place the baking sheet in the freezer for at least 2 hours or, preferably, overnight. This will help the patties keep their shape during cooking. You can also make the patties in advance and keep them in the freezer for a few days or even up to three months.

6. Once the patties are frozen and firm, remove them from the freezer and repeat the breading process: dredge each one in the flour, dip in the egg wash, then coat with the breadcrumbs.

7. Preheat the oven to 190°C/375°F/Gas 5.

8. Fill a large saucepan with 2 to 3 inches (5 to 8 centimetres) of vegetable oil, place it over medium heat, and bring the oil to between 180°C and 190°C (350°F and 375°F). Using a pair of tongs, carefully place one of the breaded patties into the hot oil. Using the tongs, turn the breaded patty over every minute or so and cook it until golden brown and crispy on all sides. Once the patty is done, transfer it to a paper-towel-lined dish and repeat the process with the remaining pieces.

9. Place the deep-fried patties on a baking-paper-lined baking sheet and bake them in the preheated oven for about 20 minutes to make sure they are cooked through on the inside.

roast duck
with banosh

Качка запечена з баношем

serves 6 to 8 | start to finish:
3 hours

pictured on pages 174–175

Roast duck is a traditional festive dish in many cuisines around the world. Ukraine is no exception, because poultry farming is very common in all regions of our country. The recipe I'm sharing here is for duck stuffed with banosh (our version of corn porridge).

1. Rub the duck both inside and outside with salt and pepper, drizzle with the oil and freshly squeezed lemon juice, and season with lemon zest. Stuff the crushed garlic cloves, sprigs of thyme, and thinly sliced chilli pepper into the duck's cavity. Cover the duck with plastic wrap and let it rest in the refrigerator for about an hour or two.

2. Prepare the banosh: combine the single and double cream, and about ½ cup (120 millilitres) cold water in a heavy saucepan, bring the mixture to a boil, and stir in the polenta. Cook at a gentle simmer for 3 to 5 minutes, whisking constantly. Remove from the heat.

3. Peel and finely mince the onion and cut the carrot and the pepper into matchsticks. Heat a little oil in a large frying pan over medium heat, add the vegetables, and sauté until tender.

4. Once the vegetables are done, stir them into the cooked polenta.

5. Stuff the polenta into the duck's cavity and carefully seal the skin shut using cocktail sticks or kitchen twine. Preheat the oven to 180°C/350°F/Gas 4. Line a baking dish with baking paper and place the duck on it.

6. Roast the stuffed duck for about 1½ hours, occasionally basting it with the pan juices.

7. Once the duck is done, let it cool slightly and serve warm.

1 whole duck, 5 to 6 pounds
  (2 to 3 kilograms)
Coarse salt and freshly ground
  black pepper
3 tablespoons sunflower oil
Juice and zest from 1 lemon
2 to 3 garlic cloves, to taste,
  crushed
5 sprigs thyme
⅓ chilli pepper, thinly sliced
½ cup (120 millilitres) single cream
½ cup (120 millilitres) double
  cream
⅔ cup (100 grams) polenta
1 large onion
1 large carrot
1 large red pepper

sautéed cabbage with prunes

Тушена капуста з чорносливом

Cabbage stewed with smoked prunes is very popular during Lent, when, in the Eastern Orthodox Church tradition, you cannot eat meat or dairy. But this dish has such a wonderful taste, you shouldn't wait for a special occasion to make it. If you want to make this dish sweeter, add some raisins along with the prunes.

1. Using a sharp knife or a mandoline, thinly slice the cabbage. Heat the butter and the sunflower oil in a large frying pan until bubbling and add the sliced cabbage. Sauté it over medium heat, stirring occasionally, until soft and golden. Season to taste with salt and freshly ground black pepper.

2. While the cabbage is cooking, wash the prunes well in warm water, remove the pits (if necessary), and chop the prunes into medium chunks. Add the prunes and the chopped walnuts to the cabbage and mix well to combine.

3. Dissolve the tomato purée in about ½ cup (120 millilitres) water and add it to the cabbage along with the freshly squeezed lemon juice and cumin. Mix everything well once more and cook over low heat until most of the liquid evaporates. Serve the cabbage warm or cold.

1 medium head white cabbage, cored
1 ounce (30 grams) unsalted butter
1 tablespoon sunflower oil (or other neutral oil)
Coarse salt and freshly ground black pepper to taste
10 large smoked prunes
⅓ cup (40 grams) chopped walnuts
1 tablespoon tomato purée
Juice of ½ lemon
Small pinch of ground cumin

beef chomber with anchovies

Чомбер з яловичини із анчоусами

When I am looking for inspiration as I research Ukraine's culinary history, I turn to the works of Olha Franko, a legendary food writer who published Ukraine's first cookbook in Kolomyia in 1929. One time, I came across two fascinating recipes that were printed on the same page. The first was for chomber, a traditional dish in which beef is soaked in vinegar and salt for about five days, then baked. The second was for oven-roasted beef with sardines. I was immediately inspired to combine them. Thinking back to the classic Italian dish vitello tonnato, I came up with a recipe for beef chomber with anchovies. Trust me, it's divine!

2½ pounds (1.2 kilograms) beef topside, cut into 6 portions
Coarse salt and freshly ground black pepper to taste
15 small anchovies or 2 salted herring fillets
½ pound (225 grams) smoked salo or bacon, thinly sliced
A few garlic cloves, crushed
A few sprigs thyme

1. Preheat the oven to 190°C/375°F/Gas 5.

2. Pat the pieces of beef dry with kitchen paper, season with salt and pepper, and set aside. Cut the anchovies or herring fillets into small pieces and wrap them in the smoked salo or bacon slices.

3. Using a sharp paring knife, make a few punctures in the steaks. Insert a piece of the salo- or bacon-wrapped anchovy or herring into most of the incisions and stuff the crushed garlic cloves into the remaining openings.

4. Heat a dry frying pan over medium-high heat and sear the steaks until nicely browned on all sides. Transfer the steaks to a medium baking dish, cover with aluminum foil, and bake for 20 to 30 minutes or until the steaks reach the desired level of doneness. Sprinkle with fresh thyme and more chopped anchovies or herring and serve warm.

braised pork with prunes

Печеня зі свинини з чорносливом

serves 6 | start to finish: *1 hour*

Prunes are a magical ingredient that add a unique taste and a rich, smoky aroma to any dish. Braised pork with prunes is a classic dish for good reason—the smoky aroma of the prunes highlights the taste of the pork. Depending on your preference, you can use lean pieces of pork or more fatty ones. If you can't find smoked prunes, you can complement the flavour of this dish with smoked paprika or smoked pear.

1½ pounds (700 grams) boneless pork shoulder, excess fat trimmed
Coarse salt and freshly ground pepper
Sunflower oil for frying
1 large onion, peeled and finely minced
1 medium carrot, diced
1 ounce (30 grams) unsalted butter
½ cup (70 grams) smoked prunes, pitted
Bay leaf

1. Cut the pork into bite-size pieces. Season lightly with salt and freshly ground pepper. Add a little sunflower oil to a large pan, heat it over medium heat, and add the pork pieces. Cook them until brown and crispy on all sides.

2. Add the onion and carrot to the pan and sauté over low heat. After a few minutes, stir in the butter.

3. Add the prunes to the pan. Add some salt and pepper and the bay leaf. Deglaze with a little water (or, better yet, vegetable or chicken broth), cover, and let simmer over low heat for about 40 minutes or until the meat is perfectly tender.

tovchanka

**mashed potatoes with
poppy seeds, peas, and beans**   *Товчанк*

If you're looking for a way to mix things up in the kitchen and you want an authentically Ukrainian version of mashed potatoes, I suggest tovchanka—mashed potatoes with poppy seeds, peas, and beans. This dish is less creamy and rich than typical cream-heavy mashed potatoes, but it is just as delicious. A must-try for all potato lovers!

½ cup (115 grams) dried split peas
½ cup (100 grams) dried white
    beans
6 medium potatoes, peeled
3 tablespoons poppy seeds
Coarse salt and freshly ground
    pepper to taste
1¾ ounces (50 grams) unsalted
    butter

1. The night before: place the split peas and the beans in separate bowls, cover with cold water, and soak overnight. (This will help them cook quicker.)

2. Dice the potatoes, add them to a large saucepan, cover with water, and bring to a boil. Reduce the heat and cook the potatoes until tender. Add the drained beans to one small saucepan, the peas to another, cover with fresh water, and bring to a boil over medium heat. Lower the heat and cook them at an easy simmer until they are soft enough to be mashed between your fingertips.

3. While the potatoes, beans, and peas are cooking, add the poppy seeds to a small bowl and soak them in scalding-hot water.

4. Drain and add the cooked potatoes, peas, and beans to a large mixing bowl, reserving some of the potato cooking water. Using a potato masher or a ricer, mash them to a thick, paste-like consistency. Mix everything well to combine.

5. Season the mashed potatoes, peas, and beans with salt and pepper. Add the drained poppy seeds and stir in the butter. Adjust the consistency by adding a little more of the potato broth.

makar

potato casserole with bacon   *Макар*

Ukrainians love potatoes, and no wonder—they're fairly easy to grow, filling, and delicious. The most popular potato dishes are, without a doubt, Deruny (page 140) and pan-fried potatoes (for example, Fried Potatoes with Goat's Cheese and Garlic, page 84), but if you travel across the country, you'll come across lesser-known but just as mouthwatering dishes, some with mysterious histories.

One of my favourite ancient and underrated potato dishes is potato makar, which I first tried in Ovruch, a city in northern Ukraine. It's a large and hearty potato casserole made with bacon and sautéed onions, one of those simple but tasty dishes that somehow end up better than the sum of their humble ingredients.

Sunflower oil
¼ cup (50 grams) cubed salo or bacon
2 medium onions, peeled and diced
2 pounds (900 grams) potatoes, peeled
Coarse salt and freshly ground black pepper

1. Preheat the oven to 190°C/375°F/Gas 5. Grease a large baking dish with a little sunflower oil.

2. Sauté the salo cubes in a dry pan over medium heat until most of the fat renders. After a few minutes, add the diced onion and sauté until fragrant and translucent. Remove the pan from the heat and set aside.

3. Using the fine side of a box grater, grate the potatoes into a sieve set over a large bowl. (This will help remove excess moisture from the potatoes.) Once you have grated all the potatoes, discard the liquid in the bowl and transfer the grated potatoes to a large mixing bowl.

4. Fold in the fried salo or bacon and onions, salt everything to taste, add a dash of freshly ground black pepper, and mix well to combine.

5. Transfer the potato mixture to the prepared baking dish. Bake the potato casserole in the preheated oven for about 30 minutes or until the surface is golden brown and a cocktail stick inserted into the centre comes out dry and clean.

varenyky with potato and cabbage fillings

Вареники з картоплею та капустою

serves 6 to 8 | start to finish:
1 hour
30 minutes

also pictured on pages 188–189

Varenyky are another of Ukraine's many signature dishes. In some regions of western Ukraine, varenyky are referred to by their Polish name: pyrohy. The dough for these stuffed dumplings can be made simply with water or with the addition of eggs and sunflower oil. Stewed cabbage, potatoes with cracklings, or meat are used as fillings.

Historically, varenyky weren't an everyday dish; they were more often prepared for Sunday meals or special occasions. No festive meal was complete without them, whether it was a wedding, a christening, or a holiday gathering.

Each household has its own fiercely guarded recipe for the dough, and there are so many varieties of fillings, from savoury to sweet, that I won't even attempt to name them all. But I do suggest you make varenyky with two of my favourite types of filling, potato and cabbage, to see just how varied this dish can be. The dough is something I've been perfecting for quite a while—it is firm enough to hold its shape and yet tender.

1. Make the dough: in a large mixing bowl, whisk together the flour and salt, stir in the egg and 3 tablespoons of oil, and slowly drizzle in a little over ¾ cup (185 millilitres) of water. Knead the dough until smooth and elastic, first oiling your hands to keep it from sticking too much. Once the dough is smooth, wrap it in plastic wrap and let rest for about 30 minutes.

2. Meanwhile, make the fillings. To make the potato filling: dice the peeled potatoes, add them to a large saucepan, cover with cold water, and bring to a boil over medium heat. Cook the potatoes at a simmer for about 20 minutes or until tender, then drain. While the potatoes are cooking, finely mince the onion and sauté it in the sunflower oil until fragrant and lightly golden. Mash the cooked potatoes, stir in the sautéed onion, season to taste, and let cool.

3. For the cabbage filling: core and finely grate the cabbage, finely mince the onion, and grate the carrot. Sauté the onion and carrot in the sunflower oil until almost done, then add the cabbage and cook everything until tender. Season to taste, transfer to a bowl, and let cool.

for the varenyky dough

3 cups (400 grams) plain flour, plus extra for dusting
Pinch of coarse salt
1 large egg
3 tablespoons sunflower oil, plus extra to grease your hands

for the potato filling

4 medium potatoes, peeled
1 large onion
2 tablespoons sunflower oil
Coarse salt and freshly ground black pepper

for the cabbage filling

1 medium head white cabbage
1 large onion
1 large carrot
2 tablespoons sunflower oil
Coarse salt and freshly ground black pepper

for garnishing

Soured cream and unsalted butter, melted
1 large onion (optional)
¼ cup (50 grams) diced bacon or salo (optional)

The Authentic Ukrainian Kitchen

4. On a lightly floured work surface, roll out the dough to approximately ¼ inch (5 millimetres) thick. Cut out rounds with a 3-inch (8-centimetre) cookie cutter or a glass. Place on a parchment-lined baking sheet and cover with plastic wrap to keep them from drying out.

5. Add about a tablespoon of one of the fillings into the centre of each dough disk until you've used up half the dough. Fold the top half down over the filling, gently press to squeeze out any air, and seal by tightly pinching the seam together. Make sure the edges are sealed tightly, otherwise they might burst during the cooking process. Then repeat with the rest of the dough using the other filling.

6. Bring a large saucepan of salted water to a boil. Working in batches, add several varenyky (the number of varenyky will depend on the size of your pot) to the boiling water and cook them for about 4 minutes or until they rise to the surface of the saucepan. Fish them out using a slotted spoon and transfer to a large bowl. Drizzle the cooked varenyky with a little oil to keep them from sticking. Repeat the process until all the varenyky are done. Divide them among serving dishes and garnish with a little soured cream, butter, or the bacon and onion mixture, below.

7. Optional garnish: finely mince the onion. In a small frying pan, render the bacon cubes over medium heat and add the onion. Sauté until the onion is golden and fragrant and the bacon bits are nice and crispy. Spoon over the cooked varenyky.

Sweets

blackcurrant jam

Варення з смородини

makes two 8-fluid ounce (225 millilitre) jars | start to finish: *30 minutes*

Back in the old days, jams and jellies did more than just satisfy people's cravings for something sweet—they were also a way to preserve fruit throughout the cold months. That's why each summer, Ukrainians flock to the markets to buy fresh berries or pick them in their own gardens if they have them, then spend a weekend or two making jam out of the ripe, sweet berries, filling the entire kitchen with a mouthwatering smell. In the winter, when the jam jars are taken out of the fridges or cellars and opened, the whole family is reminded of warm, sunny summer days. So if you see fresh blackcurrants at the market, make sure to try my mother's favourite recipe for blackcurrant jam!

Following this recipe, you can prepare jam from raspberries, blackberries, or blueberries, depending on your preference.

2¼ pounds (1 kilogram) blackcurrants
2½ cups (500 grams) granulated sugar
A few whole black peppercorns, to taste

1. Rinse the blackcurrants well in cold water and transfer them to a large heavy-based saucepan. Add the sugar, mix to combine, and let the mixture rest for about 10 minutes; this will help the blackcurrants release their juices.

2. Bring the mixture to a boil over low heat and cook, stirring often, for about 15 minutes or until the sugar has fully dissolved and the mixture has thickened.

3. Using the flat side of a large chef's knife, crush the black peppercorns. Add them, little by little, to the saucepan, tasting as you go. Once you have reached your desired level of heat, simmer the jam for another minute and remove from the heat. Let cool before serving. The jam can be stored in the refrigerator in a closed jar for up to 3 months.

apricot jam with walnuts

Варення з абрикосів із волоськими горіхами

makes three to four 8-fluid ounce (225 milli-litre) jars

start to finish: *45 minutes*

Here's another jam recipe that comes from my family's cookbook. Every summer, my mother picks apricots from her garden and makes a thick, fragrant jam that's beloved by everyone in the family. I played around with her recipe and added some chopped walnuts, which enhance the jam's texture and highlight its deep, rich flavour.

2¼ pounds (1 kilogram) fresh apricots
2½ cups (500 grams) granulated sugar
¾ cup (100 grams) chopped walnuts
Several 8-fluid ounce (225 millilitre) glass jars, sterilized (see note on page 12)

1. Wash the apricots, discard any spoiled ones, and remove the stones. Cut the apricots in half and lay them, skin-side up, on a baking-paper-lined baking sheet. (This will remove the excess moisture from the apricots.) After about 15 minutes, transfer the apricot halves to a large, heavy-based pot. Add the sugar and let the apricots rest for about 10 minutes or until they release their juices and the sugar dissolves a little.

2. Bring the apricots to a boil over medium heat, stirring constantly. Reduce the heat to medium-low and stir in the chopped walnuts. Cook the jam for at least 10 minutes, occasionally stirring it and discarding any foam.

3. Divide the hot jam among freshly sterilized jars, making sure the jars are also hot or at least warm; they might crack if they are too cold. Put the lids on the jars and let them cool completely at room temperature before transferring them to the fridge.

rose-petal and lemon jam

Варення з ружі

makes one 16-fluid ounce (450 millilitre) or two 8-fluid ounce (225 millilitre) jars	start to finish: *11 hours 40 minutes*

There is some evidence that Lesya Ukrainka—a famous Ukrainian poet born in Volyn and known for her romantic works filled with allusions to Ukrainian folklore—made this rose-petal jam. It's hard to find concrete evidence for this, but I like to believe she did—besides, the recipe for this jam can be found in Ukrainian cookbooks from her time in the nineteenth century. Its taste is magical, as if it were cooked by fairies right out of a fairy tale. If you haven't tried it yet, now is the time.

7 ounces (200 grams) fresh edible tea-rose petals
1 cup plus 1 tablespoon (212 grams) granulated sugar
Zest and juice from ½ lemon
1¼ cups (275 millilitres) water
1 teaspoon fruit pectin (optional)

1. Lightly dust any dirt off the rose petals and discard any that are dry or browned. Working in batches, rinse the petals well and transfer them to a deep bowl. Cover them with about a cup (250 millilitres) of scalding-hot water. After a few seconds, carefully drain the hot water and transfer the blanched petals to a medium saucepan.

2. Add ½ cup (100 grams) of the sugar, the lemon juice, and the lemon zest to the saucepan with the petals. Set the pan aside.

3. In a separate small saucepan, combine the water and ½ cup (100 grams) of the sugar, saving the rest of the sugar to combine with the pectin later if using. Bring the mixture to a gentle simmer over medium heat and let it cook until it thickens into a runny but sticky syrup.

4. Once the syrup is ready, add it to the pan with the rose petals and let rest at room temperature for at least 4 hours.

5. Bring the syrup and petals to a boil over medium heat, reduce the heat, and cook, covered, for about 5 minutes. Then remove from the heat and let cool for 6 hours. If you prefer runny jam, when it has cooled completely, blitz it using a blender, transfer it to a sterile jar, and store it in the fridge for up to ten months.

6. If you prefer thicker jam, whisk together the pectin and 1 tablespoon of sugar in a small bowl. Blitz the jam in a blender, bring it to a simmer in a saucepan placed over medium heat, stir in the sugar and pectin mixture, and let the jam come to a rolling boil. Let it cook for 5 more minutes, then remove it from the heat. Transfer it into a 16-fluid ounce (450 millilitre) sterile jar (or several smaller ones), let cool, and store in the fridge for up to ten months.

kiflyky

jam-filled crescent pastries   *Кіфлики*

A kiflyk is a sweet crescent-shaped pastry that is very popular in
Zakarpattia. It looks like a small croissant but is made of regular
dough rather than puff pastry. How this recipe became part of
Ukraine's culinary tradition is mysterious; some associate it with
Austrian cultural influences, while others mention Turkish roots, due
to its crescent shape. Regardless of its origins, the kiflyk is integral to
Ukrainian cuisine. Traditionally, kiflyky are stuffed with thick plum
jam. You can use any kind of jam or preserve, but it must be thick.

1. In a medium mixing bowl, whisk together both types of flour. Using
   the coarse side of a box grater, grate the very cold butter and add it
   to the mixing bowl. Using your hands, rub the butter into the flour
   mixture until you get a crumbly mixture resembling slightly moist sand.
   Add the sugar, the salt, and the egg. Mix well to combine.

2. In a small mixing bowl, combine the soured cream and the yeast. If you
   have a stand mixer with a dough-hook attachment, transfer the dough
   to the bowl of the stand mixer and add the soured cream and yeast. If
   not, simply add the soured cream and yeast to the dough and mix until
   combined.

3. Using a dough-hook attachment or your hands, knead the dough until
   smooth and elastic. If the dough looks dry, feel free to add a little more
   soured cream. If it gets too soft, add a little more flour. The consistency
   should be soft and pliable. Once the dough has reached the desired
   consistency, take it out of the bowl, wrap tightly in plastic wrap, and let
   rest in the refrigerator for an hour.

4. While the dough is resting, make the filling: in a small mixing bowl,
   combine the plum preserves with the chopped walnuts and poppy
   seeds. Line a baking sheet with baking paper and preheat the oven to
   200°C/400°F/Gas 6.

5. Take the dough out of the fridge and divide it in half. Roll each half
   into a ball, flatten it, and roll it out into a flat disk approximately
   8 inches (20 centimetres) in diameter. Slice each dough disk into 8 to
   10 triangular segments. Put about a tablespoon of the filling on the
   wider side of each segment. Starting from the wide end, roll up and
   twist each dough triangle into a crescent-shaped roll.

6. Transfer the rolls to the parchment-lined baking sheet, making sure
   they are at least ½ inch (1 centimetre) apart; if necessary, bake them in
   batches. Whisk the egg yolk in a small bowl and, using a silicone brush,
   brush a little of the yolk onto each crescent roll. Sprinkle each roll with
   a little sugar.

7. Bake the rolls in the preheated oven for about 20 minutes or until
   golden and crispy. Dust the baked rolls with a little icing sugar.

**makes 16 to
20 kiflyky**   **start to finish:
*1 hour
30 minutes***

for the pastry

2½ cups (340 grams) strong bread
  flour
1 cup (260 grams) corn flour
7½ ounces (215 grams) unsalted
  butter, cold
3 tablespoons granulated sugar
Pinch of coarse salt
1 large egg
1½ cups (350 millilitres) soured
  cream
2¼ teaspoons (7 grams) easy-
  bake/fast-action yeast
1 large egg yolk
Brown sugar (optional)

for the filling

¾ cup (220 grams) thick plum jam
3 tablespoons chopped walnuts
3 tablespoons poppy seeds
Icing sugar for serving

paska

traditional easter bread   *Паска*

makes 2 large
paskas

start to finish:
*4 hours
40 minutes*

According to Ukrainian tradition, everyone celebrating Easter should start the holiday meal with a nice large piece of paska (special Easter bread) that was blessed by a priest during the Easter morning service. There's some debate about which type of paska is the most authentic—back in the day, many Ukrainians made a soft cheese–based paska for the holiday, while nowadays, most prefer a dough-based sweet paska resembling panettone.

Making paska is a special endeavor that calls for patience and concentration. It's said that when you make paska, you shouldn't even talk loudly. Another key to a successful outcome is kneading the dough. The longer it's kneaded, the fluffier the paska will be. It's better to do it with your hands, because the warmth of your hands helps activate the yeast, but your kitchen mixer can also do the job (I suggest using low speeds for kneading).

¾ cup (100 grams) raisins
1 cup (250 millilitres) warm milk
1 ounce (30 grams) fresh yeast (or
   2¼ teaspoons/7 grams easy-
   bake/fast-action yeast)
1 cup (200 grams) granulated
   sugar plus 1 tablespoon
   for the starter
1 large egg
1 large egg yolk
2 tablespoons soured cream
1¼ ounces (35 grams) vanilla sugar
4 ounces (115 grams) unsalted
   butter, cubed and softened to
   room temperature
Coarse salt
6 cups (800 grams) strong bread
   flour
1½ tablespoons cognac
2 tablespoons sunflower oil
1 cup (140 grams) icing sugar
Juice from ½ orange
Sprinkles (if desired)

1. Thoroughly wash the raisins, soak them in about a cup (250 millilitres) of hot water, and set aside.

2. Make the starter: in a medium saucepan, heat the milk until slightly warm to the touch and whisk in the yeast. Mix well and sprinkle a tablespoon of granulated sugar over the mixture. Mix once more, then cover the pan with a kitchen towel and let rest in a warm place for about 20 minutes or until the mixture becomes foamy and doubles in size. Once it does, stir in the whole egg and the egg yolk.

3. Transfer the starter to a large mixing bowl and stir in the remaining sugar, the soured cream, the vanilla sugar, the cubed and softened butter, and a pinch of salt. Mix everything thoroughly, then gradually add in the flour and the cognac. Keep mixing everything with a wooden spoon until a shaggy dough forms. After that, knead it out using your hands until elastic and tacky.

4. Shape the dough into a ball and transfer it to a large bowl generously greased with sunflower oil. Cover it with a kitchen towel and let the dough rest in a warm place for about an hour or until it doubles in size.

5. Knead the dough out once more to deflate it, shape it into a ball, and place it back into the well-oiled bowl. Cover with a kitchen towel and let rest in a warm, draft-free place for another 40 minutes. This process is called double-proofing, and it is the secret to fluffy, tender paska.

6. Once you have proofed the dough for a second time, take it out of the bowl and, using your hands, press it onto a lightly floured kitchen surface. Drain the raisins, sprinkle them onto the dough, and knead it just long enough to incorporate them evenly. Try to keep most of the

recipe continues

raisins inside the dough and not on its surface, as they might burn during baking.

7. Divide the dough into 2 equal parts and place each portion of dough into a 9-inch (23-centimetre) baking-paper-lined baking mould (the moulds should be filled about two-thirds of the way up). Cover the moulds, put them in a warm, draft-free place, and let rest for about 20 minutes or until the moulds are almost full of the rising dough. Meanwhile, preheat the oven to 180°C/350°F/Gas 4.

8. Bake the paskas in the preheated oven for 30 to 35 minutes or until the tops are golden brown. After baking, let them cool completely and make the glaze: in a medium bowl, whisk together the orange juice and the icing sugar until smooth and thick. Pour the glaze over each cooled paska. If you like, cover the tops of the paskas with colourful sprinkles before the glaze sets.

cherry torte with walnuts

Пляцок з вишнями та волоськими горіхами

makes one
9-inch
(23-centimetre)
torte

start to finish:
50 minutes

pictured on pages 204–205

Dessert pastries made with fresh cherries are an ancient Ukrainian culinary tradition. They appear in all different forms, from rolls to regular pies, and are made with various types of dough, including yeast dough, bicarbonate of soda dough, and baking-powder dough. But they all have one thing in common—they are incredibly tasty. This torte recipe is very easy; all you have to do is make a simple cake dough, mix it with cherries, and let the oven work its magic. Since the dough is quite sweet, a crispy caramel crust forms on the surface of the finished torte, which is simply irresistible.

2 large eggs
1 scant cup (180 grams) sugar
1 teaspoon vanilla sugar (or a drop or two of vanilla extract)
1 cup (130 grams) plain flour
1 teaspoon baking powder
Small pinch of coarse salt
1 cup (110 grams) chopped walnuts
1 pound (450 grams) pitted fresh or frozen cherries (if using frozen cherries, thaw them completely)

1. Preheat the oven to 190°C/375°F/Gas 5.

2. In a medium mixing bowl, whisk the eggs, the sugar, and the vanilla sugar until smooth and creamy.

3. In a second bowl, sift together the flour and baking powder. Add the salt and whisk well to combine.

4. Fold the dry ingredients into the egg mixture and mix until smooth. Fold in the chopped walnuts and the cherries.

5. Line a 9-inch (23-centimetre) round or 9- by 13-inch (23- by 33-centimetre) baking dish with baking paper. Pour the batter into the lined dish and bake the torte in the preheated oven for about 40 minutes or until a cocktail stick inserted into the centre comes out clean and only barely moist. Let the torte cool in the baking dish before serving.

lamantsi

crunchy cakes with poppy seeds   *Ламанці*

Mentions of crunchy cakes with poppy-seed sauce can be found in Ukrainian literature from the twentieth century. In some regions, this dish was known as shulyky. Traditionally, lamantsi were made with unleavened dough for the Makoviy—an Eastern Orthodox feast with ancient folk roots that is associated with the start of the harvest and the gathering of honey. I suggest making the dough with eggs and butter so it is fluffy and flavourful. Lamantsi are perfect for holidays and festive occasions—family members can gather around the table and share a large bowl of these broken cakes with the poppy-seed sauce.

1. Preheat the oven to 190°C/375°F/Gas 5.

2. Make the dough: in a medium bowl, whisk together the flour, sugar, poppy seeds, baking powder, a pinch of salt, and cumin. Add the cubed butter (make sure it is as cold as possible) and, using your hands, rub the butter into the flour mixture until the texture resembles wet sand and no big lumps of butter remain.

3. Stir in the egg and the soured cream. Using your hands, knead the dough until it becomes tacky, smooth and firm. If the dough is too soft, add a little more flour and knead it a little more.

4. Place a large sheet of baking parchment on your kitchen surface and place the dough into the centre. Cover it with another layer of baking parchment and roll the dough out into a rectangle about a tenth of an inch (2 millimetres) thick. Remove the top layer of parchment and, using a fork, poke holes in the rolled-out dough. Transfer it to a baking sheet together with the bottom layer of the parchment and bake in the preheated oven for about 15 minutes or until golden. Halfway through baking, remove the dough from the oven and flip it over.

5. While the dough is in the oven, make the poppy-seed dip: in a small saucepan, whisk together the milk, poppy seeds, honey, and cinnamon. Bring the mixture to a gentle simmer and cook for 5 to 10 minutes or until it thickens enough to coat the back of a spoon. Remove from the heat.

6. Remove the baked poppy-seed cake from the oven and let cool a little before breaking it into small pieces. Serve with the poppy-seed dip.

for the dough

2 cups (260 grams) plain flour, plus extra for dusting
½ cup (100 grams) granulated sugar
1 tablespoon poppy seeds
½ teaspoon baking powder
Coarse salt
Generous pinch of ground cumin
2½ ounces (70 grams) unsalted butter, cubed and very cold
1 large egg
3½ fluid ounces (100 millilitres) soured cream

for the poppy-seed dip

1 cup (250 millilitres) milk
3 tablespoons poppy seeds
2 tablespoons honey
1 teaspoon ground cinnamon

medivnyk

honey layer cake   *Медівник*

This honey layer cake is a classic dessert beloved by kids and adults
alike. Adding honey to the cake batter gives the cake a gorgeous
golden colour, and the soured cream–based frosting is the perfect
balance of sweet and slightly sour. Cake decorations are made from
leftover dough that's baked and then crumbled with a rolling pin or in
a blender.

You can buy this cake in pretty much any grocery store or bakery in
Ukraine, but I believe that the tastiest medivnyk is the one you make
at home and proudly share with your loved ones.

Medivnyk is also the name for regular cookies made with honey
that children were traditionally treated with on Christmas and New
Year's. But I think you might like the cake version better.

1. Start the soured cream frosting: first, remove the excess liquid from the
   soured cream. To do this, place several layers of muslin in a colander
   and spoon the soured cream onto the muslin. Place the colander
   over a bowl and let the excess liquid filter through and into the bowl.
   I suggest letting the soured cream rest like this overnight (in the fridge,
   of course) or for at least a few hours.

2. For the cake: in a medium bowl, whisk together the three eggs and
   the bicarbonate of soda. Set aside.

3. In a heatproof bowl placed over a saucepan of simmering water, whisk
   together the butter, honey, sugar, and salt until they come together
   to form a sticky, smooth mixture. Slowly drizzle in the egg mixture,
   making sure the bowl doesn't get too hot so the eggs don't start to
   curdle. Cook the mixture for about 5 minutes or until it thickens
   enough to coat the back of a spoon.

4. Remove the mixture from the heat and fold in the flour. Whisk the
   batter until no lumps of flour remain and a smooth dough forms,
   then cover the bowl with plastic wrap and let it rest in the fridge for
   1½ hours.

5. Preheat the oven to 180°C/350°F/Gas 4.

6. Remove the dough from the fridge and divide it into 8 equal parts.
   On a kitchen surface lightly dusted with flour, roll each one out into
   a rectangle about ⅛ inch (3 millimetres) thick and at least 6 inches
   (15 centimetres) on one side, trimming the edges with a sharp knife. To
   create matching dough rounds, you can place a 6-inch (15-centimetre)
   cake pan upside down over each layer of dough and trace the shape
   with a knife before trimming. Don't discard the scraps; we'll need them
   to make the crumb topping.

**makes one
6-inch
(15-centimetre)
cake**

start to finish:
*3 hours
to overnight,
plus 2 hours
10 minutes*

---

pictured on pages 210–211

---

for the soured cream frosting

2¾ cups (650 millilitres) soured
   cream
¾ cup plus 1½ tablespoons
   (200 millilitres) double cream
1¼ cups (175 grams) icing sugar

for the cake

3 medium eggs
1 teaspoon bicarbonate of soda
4 ounces (115 grams) unsalted
   butter
3 tablespoons honey
½ cup (100 grams) sugar
⅓ teaspoon salt
3½ cups (460 grams) plain flour

7. Bake the layers of dough and scraps two at a time on a baking-paper-lined baking sheet for 6 to 7 minutes. Let each layer cool after baking and repeat the process with the remaining layers and the saved scraps of dough.

8. To make the frosting, whip the double cream until fluffy. In a separate bowl, whisk together the drained soured cream and the icing sugar. Gently fold the whipped cream into the soured cream mixture, taking care not to overmix.

9. Assemble the cake: Spread a generous amount of frosting onto one of the cake layers, then top with another layer of cake and another generous portion of frosting. Don't skimp on the frosting—the cake will absorb a lot of it. Repeat the process with the remaining layers of cake and the rest of the frosting. Once you're done with the assembly, make the crumb topping: blitz the baked cake scraps in a food processor or crumble them with a rolling pin, then cover the sides and top of the cake with the crumbs.

10. Let the cake rest in the fridge overnight before serving.

kutya

serves 4 | start to finish: *Overnight, plus 3 hours*

festive sweet wheat porridge   *Кутя*

Ukrainians who celebrate Christmas have very specific traditions. For instance, when the first star comes out on Christmas Eve, the whole family gathers around a table filled with twelve different dishes. All the dishes have to be Lenten (meaning free of any meat or dairy), and the real star of the meal is kutya—a sweet festive porridge served at room temperature and garnished with honey, chopped nuts, dried fruit, and poppy seeds. The specific ingredients added to kutya vary depending on the region, but the dish's symbolic importance is the same all over the country.

Kutya—along with other dishes and a sheaf of wheat used as a centrepiece on Christmas Eve—was a symbol of the harvest. The meal was supposed to start with kutya, and kutya was taken as a gift to relatives on the second day of Christmas.

But despite the sacred meaning of kutya, you don't have to wait until Christmas to make it. Historically, kutya was made with whole-grain wheat, but now you can find versions with rice or pearl barley.

1 cup (160 grams) wheat berries
1 ounce (30 grams) unsalted butter
½ cup (85 grams) dried apricots
¼ cup (35 grams) walnuts
¼ cup (40 grams) raisins
2 tablespoons poppy seeds
2 to 3 tablespoons honey, to taste
Juice from ½ large lemon, or to taste

1. Soak the wheat berries overnight in a large mixing bowl filled with cold water. Make sure you add plenty of water, since the wheat will absorb it as it soaks.

2. Drain and rinse the soaked wheat, transfer it to a medium saucepan, cover with 4 cups (1 litre) fresh cold water, and bring to a boil over medium-high heat. Reduce the heat a little and cook at a gentle simmer, uncovered, for about an hour or until the wheat becomes soft. The water should have evaporated by then, but if it hasn't, drain the wheat once more. Stir in the butter and set aside.

3. Finely chop the dried apricots and walnuts. Transfer the cooked wheat to a large bowl and stir in the apricots, walnuts, raisins, and poppy seeds. Add the honey and adjust the sweetness of the dish according to your taste by adding a little freshly squeezed lemon juice. Transfer the kutya to the fridge and let it rest for at least 2 hours to help the flavours meld together.

verhuny

Вергуни

Verhuny or, as they are sometimes called, khrustyky (meaning "crisps") are an unfairly forgotten Ukrainian dessert. I'm sure that with a little marketing and some good PR, these deep-fried pieces of sweet dough could become just as popular as doughnuts. Traditionally, verhuny were cooked for vechornytsi (traditional Ukrainian gatherings with music, songs, jokes, and rituals), to treat carolers during holidays, and even during fasting periods.

I can't imagine why these golden crispy treats have fallen out of fashion, as they truly are a wonderful dessert. Some of you may be afraid of deep-frying, but believe me, it isn't as complicated as it seems. Try them out before they go mainstream!

3 cups (400 grams) plain flour

1¾ ounces (50 grams) unsalted butter, cubed and softened

½ teaspoon bicarbonate of soda

½ cup (120 millilitres) soured cream

1 large egg

3 large egg yolks

¼ cup (50 grams) granulated sugar

1 tablespoon apple cider vinegar

Coarse salt

3 cups (700 millilitres) neutral oil, for frying

1 cup (140 grams) icing sugar

1. In a large mixing bowl, combine the flour, softened butter, and bicarbonate of soda using a spatula. Mix in the soured cream, whole egg, egg yolks, granulated sugar, apple cider vinegar, and salt. Mix with a wooden spoon until well combined, then use your hands to knead into a smooth and elastic dough. Wrap it in plastic wrap and let it rest in the fridge for about 20 minutes.

2. Turn the dough out onto a well-floured surface and roll it into a thin sheet. Using a sharp knife or a pizza cutter, cut the dough first into 2-inch-wide (5-centimetre) strips and then slice across it a few times diagonally so that you end up with diamond shapes of dough. Make a 1¼-inch (3-centimetre) incision in the centre of each diamond and pull one of the ends through the cut.

3. Heat the oil in a large heavy-based pot to about 320°F/160°C. Carefully lower a few of the dough diamonds into the hot oil and cook them until they rise to the surface, about 2 minutes. Fish them out with a slotted spoon and arrange on a large plate lined with kitchen paper. Generously dust the deep-fried pastry with the icing sugar while they are hot and repeat the process with the remaining dough. Serve the pastries warm and eat immediately.

kurabiye

shortbread cookies with jam   *Кхурабіе*

makes about
1 pound
(450 grams)
cookies

start to finish:
50 minutes

This pastry dates back to ancient Persia, and it became popular in
Ukraine thanks to Crimean Tatars, who baked it mainly for special
occasions, especially weddings. You can also find kurabiye among the
Greeks, who consider it one of their national dishes.

Recipes for this cookie vary by region. The shape of the pastry varies
too, from the familiar round flower shape with a drop of jam in the
middle to a simple circle or an oval resembling a flower petal. The
pastries can be large, resembling the size of regular cookies, or small,
about the size of a coin. Personally, I prefer the latter, and I'd like to
share this recipe with you.

for the jam

¾ cup (90 grams) fresh or thawed
frozen cranberries
½ cup (100 grams) granulated
sugar

for the shortbread cookies

3 large egg whites
2¾ ounces (75 grams) icing sugar
5½ ounces (150 grams) unsalted
butter
1¾ cups (230 grams) plain flour
2¼ teaspoons vanilla sugar (or a
drop or two of vanilla extract)

1. Make the cranberry jam: in a small saucepan, whisk together the
    cranberries and sugar and bring them to a boil over medium heat.
    Reduce the heat and let the mixture simmer for about 15 minutes or
    until it is thick enough to coat the back of a spoon. Stir the mixture
    from time to time so it won't burn. Once the jam has thickened to your
    liking, remove it from the heat and let cool completely.

2. Preheat the oven to 455°F/235°C. Make sure the oven is fully
    preheated before baking; if it is too cool, the cookies may spread out
    and lose their shape.

3. Make the cookie batter: in a medium bowl, whisk together the egg
    whites and the icing sugar until foamy. Melt the butter in a saucepan
    over low heat, making sure not to let it burn. Let it cool for about a
    minute. In a separate bowl, mix the melted butter and the flour with
    a wooden spoon until smooth, then fold in the egg white and sugar
    mixture, taking care not to overmix. Whisk in the vanilla sugar and
    carefully mix the dough with a silicone spatula until smooth.

4. Using slightly wet hands, knead the pastry dough until it is smooth and
    elastic, about 5 minutes. Transfer it to a pastry bag. On a baking sheet
    lined with baking paper, squeeze out little circles of batter (the size of
    the cookies will depend on the size of the nozzle you use). Place about
    ½ teaspoon of cranberry jam in the centre of each one.

5. Bake the cookies in the preheated oven for 7 to 10 minutes, depending
    on their size, until they are golden brown and crisp on the outside.
    Remove the finished cookies from the oven and let them cool on the
    baking sheet before serving. It's best to eat them immediately, but you
    can store them in a cookie jar for a week or so.

yevhen's plyatsok

chocolate and cherry cake   *Пляцок від Євгена*

In central Ukraine, the word *plyatsok* denotes a flatbread or a pancake, but people in western Ukraine use it to describe a layer cake made of sponge cake covered with cream or drenched in syrup. Like any other layer cake, this one looks stunning and isn't that difficult to make—all you need to do is follow the instructions and have a little patience. To be honest, I don't know where this specific recipe originated or how authentic this interpretation is, but I do know it's absolutely mouthwatering, and you need to make it for yourself.

Make sure that you're using good-quality dark chocolate (at least 55 percent cocoa) and good-quality butter (82 percent fat). This will make your cake taste truly decadent and rich.

for the cake

1¼ cups (180 grams) finely chopped dark chocolate
6 large eggs
¾ cup (150 grams) granulated sugar
5½ ounces (150 grams) unsalted butter, plus extra for greasing
1 cup minus 2 tablespoons (110 grams) icing sugar
¼ cup (50 grams) vanilla sugar
1 cup (130 grams) plain flour

1. Preheat the oven to 190°C/375°F/Gas 5.

2. For the cake: place the finely chopped chocolate in a heatproof bowl set over a pan of simmering water. The bottom of the bowl should not touch the surface of the water, and the water itself should stay at a gentle simmer. When the chocolate is completely melted, remove the bowl and set it aside.

3. Separate the egg whites from the yolks and place in separate bowls. I recommend separating each egg into two small cups before adding the white and the yolk to their respective bowls. Make sure the bowl for the egg whites is completely dry, clean, and free of any traces of oil.

4. In a small bowl, combine the granulated sugar and the egg whites and beat them to stiff peaks. You can do this by hand or using a stand mixer with a whisk attachment.

5. In a medium bowl, cream together the butter, icing sugar, and vanilla sugar. Whisk in the egg yolks and mix until smooth, then carefully stir in the melted chocolate. Carefully fold in the egg whites, making sure not to overmix, as this will deflate the batter. Using a rubber spatula, fold in the flour until just combined.

6. Transfer the batter to a small springform cake pan generously greased with butter and dusted with a little flour. Place in the preheated oven and bake for 20 minutes. The cake is ready when a wooden tester inserted into the centre comes out clean.

7. Meanwhile, make the cherry filling: Combine the cherries and sugar in a small saucepan, place it over medium heat, and bring to a gentle simmer. Cook until the sugar completely dissolves and the mixture begins to thicken a little. Take off the heat and set aside.

8. In a separate saucepan, make the glaze: combine the sugar, ⅓ cup (80 millilitres) water, and the chocolate and cook the mixture over low heat until it comes together and becomes smooth and glossy. Stir in the butter and remove from the heat.

9. Once the sponge cake has baked through, remove it from the oven and let cool in the pan for 5 to 10 minutes. Turn out onto a cooling rack and let cool completely, about 15 minutes, and then carefully slice it in half horizontally to create two disks.

10. Spread the cherry filling evenly on top of one of the sponge cake halves. Place the second half on top of the filling and lightly press down. Pour the chocolate glaze over the cake, evening it out with an offset spatula. Let cool completely before serving.

for the cherry filling

1½ cups (250 grams) fresh or frozen cherries, pitted
¾ cup (150 grams) granulated sugar

for the glaze

½ cup (100 grams) granulated sugar
½ cup (70 grams) finely chopped dark chocolate
3¼ ounces (90 grams) unsalted butter

tertyi pyrig

shortcrust pastry bars   *Тертий пиріг*

Ukrainians call this dish tertyi pyrig ("grated pie") and it's similar to a shortcrust pastry bar, especially since it's cut into rectangles before serving. This dessert is extremely popular because of its simplicity (it comes together in no time and is made with pantry staples) and its lovely taste. If you ever need to whip up a dessert when unexpected guests arrive on your doorstep, I suggest you make this one.

1. Make the filling: combine the fresh or frozen berries and the sugar in a small heavy-based saucepan and bring to a boil over medium heat, stirring constantly so the berries don't stick to the bottom of the pan. Reduce the heat and let the mixture cook at a simmer until it thickens. To check if the jam is done, take a teaspoon of jam from the saucepan and place it on a cold plate. If the jam is ready, it should stick to the plate and not be too runny when you tilt the plate from side to side. If the filling is still too runny, simmer it for a few more minutes. Once it is done, stir in the chopped basil leaves, simmer it for a minute more, and remove from the heat.

2. For the pastry: In a medium bowl, cream the softened butter with the granulated sugar, the salt, and the vanilla sugar until fluffy. You can do this using a whisk or a mixer fitted with a whisking attachment. Whisk in the two eggs. In a separate bowl, combine the flour and the baking powder. Stir the dry ingredients into the butter-and-egg mixture and mix until well combined. Using your hands, knead the dough until it is smooth and elastic. Roll the dough into a ball and divide it into two unequal parts—one-third of the dough will be used for the base and the remaining two-thirds will be used for the topping. Wrap both portions of the dough separately in plastic wrap and place the larger one in the freezer and the smaller one in the fridge. Let both rest for 30 minutes.

3. Preheat the oven to 190°C/375°F/Gas 5. Place the smaller piece of dough between two sheets of baking paper and, using a rolling pin, roll it out into a large rectangle. Remove the top piece of baking paper and transfer the dough along with the lower piece of parchment onto a baking sheet. Cover the rolled-out dough with an even, generous layer of the homemade jam.

4. Remove the second part of the dough from the freezer and unwrap it. Using a box grater, grate all the frozen dough onto the jam-covered base. The jam should still be visible through the layer of grated dough, but it should also be evenly covered. If needed, spread the grated dough more evenly using your hands.

5. Place the baking sheet with the pastry into the preheated oven and bake for 25 to 30 minutes or until the crust becomes golden brown and crispy. Let the pastry cool completely before cutting it into individual bars.

for the jam filling

1 pound (450 grams) fresh or frozen blackcurrants (or other berries, such as blueberries)
1 cup (200 grams) granulated sugar
Leaves from 5 sprigs purple basil, chopped

for the pastry

8½ ounces (240 grams) unsalted butter, cubed and brought to room temperature
1¼ cups (250 grams) granulated sugar
Pinch of coarse salt
¼ cup (50 grams) vanilla sugar (or a drop or two of vanilla extract)
2 large eggs
3⅓ cups (440 grams) plain flour
2 teaspoons baking powder

lvivsky syrnyk

makes one 6-inch (15-centimetre) cheesecake	start to finish: 2 hours 40 minutes

Lviv cheesecake with chocolate glaze   *Львівський сирник*

Some sources claim that the Lviv syrnyk was invented by Daria Zweck, a famous cook, baker, and cookbook author from the Galicia region (now Ivano-Frankivsk, Lviv, and Ternopil). However, most culinary historians note that similar recipes have long been used in traditional Galician cooking and can be found in ancient records from the region. It's a wonderful and easy dessert, whatever its history. And don't be alarmed by the fact that this recipe calls for potatoes—they make the cheesecake even more fluffy and creamy. The key to this dessert is to mix the soft cheese and potato mixture thoroughly until smooth.

1. Preheat the oven to 190°C/375°F/Gas 5. Place the potatoes in a medium saucepan and cover with cold water. Bring to a boil over medium heat. Reduce the heat a little. Let the potatoes cook at a steady rolling boil until tender, about 20 minutes.

2. Place the soft cheese in a large bowl. Add the eggs, butter, flour, and sugar. Mix well with an immersion blender until the mixture is creamy and fluffy.

3. Once the potatoes have cooked through, let them cool down in a bowl of cold water. Once they are cool enough to handle, peel them. Using a Microplane or a box grater with small holes, grate the peeled potatoes and add them to the cheese and sugar mixture. (Alternatively, you can put them through a ricer.) Mix well to combine and gently fold in the dried apricots and raisins.

4. Line the base of a 6-inch (15-centimetre) cake pan with baking parchment. Grease the sides of the pan with butter and lightly dust with flour. Pour the cheesecake batter into the pan and even out the top with a spatula or spoon.

5. Bake the cheesecake in the preheated oven for 60 to 70 minutes or until the top is golden brown and a cocktail stick inserted in the centre comes out clean and dry. Let cool in the pan on a wire rack completely before glazing with the chocolate mixture.

6. Make the chocolate glaze: fill a small saucepan with water and place a heatproof bowl on top of it so the base of the bowl is not directly touching the water. Place the makeshift double boiler over medium heat. Bring the water to a simmer, turn off the heat, and add the chopped dark chocolate to the bowl. Let it sit until almost completely melted, then add the cold butter. Once everything has melted, whisk to combine into a glossy dark glaze.

7. Carefully flip the cheesecake upside down onto a serving tray. Pour the glaze over the whole cheesecake. Use a spatula or a spoon to spread it out evenly on all sides.

for the cheesecake

10 ounces (280 grams) starchy potatoes, whole and unpeeled
3½ cups (800 grams) full-fat soft cheese
4 large eggs
2⅛ ounces (60 grams) unsalted butter, room temperature, plus more for greasing
2 tablespoons plain flour
1 cup (200 grams) granulated sugar
½ cup (85 grams) dried apricots, roughly chopped
½ cup (80 grams) raisins

for the chocolate glaze

10 ounces (150 grams) good-quality dark chocolate, chopped
2⅛ ounces (60 grams) unsalted butter, cold

syrna babka

serves 4 to 6 | start to finish: *1 hour 10 minutes*

soft cheese cake   *Сирна бабка*

Syrna babka is the Ukrainian answer to American cheesecake.
Recipes for syrna babka can be found in cookbooks from the early
twentieth century, but similar recipes probably existed even earlier.
Nowadays, this dish is often called syrna zapikanka (meaning "soft
cheese casserole") because it's baked in the oven. Many recipes mix
soft cheese with whole eggs or egg yolks, but I suggest whisking the
egg whites separately and then adding them. Trust me, this trick works
wonders—it makes the syrna babka turn out incredibly airy and
tender. For a twist, you can add diced dried apricots or figs along
with the raisins.

1. Preheat the oven to 190°C/375°F/Gas 5.

2. In a large mixing bowl, whisk together the soft cheese, egg yolks,
   soured cream, granulated sugar, vanilla sugar, flour, and salt until
   smooth. Fold in the raisins.

3. In a separate bowl, whisk the egg whites until they form soft peaks.
   Using a rubber spatula, carefully fold the fluffy egg whites into the soft
   cheese mixture. Be gentle, otherwise the egg whites might deflate!

4. Generously grease a baking dish with the butter and dust it with a little
   flour. Pour in the soft cheese mixture and even it out with a spatula if
   needed.

5. Place the baking dish into the preheated oven and bake for 45 to
   50 minutes. Let cool before slicing into individual pieces, dusting each
   one with a little icing sugar.

2¼ cups (500 grams) soft cheese
4 large eggs, whites and yolks
  separated
⅓ cup (80 millilitres) soured cream
1 cup (200 grams) granulated
  sugar
2 teaspoons vanilla sugar (or a few
  drops of vanilla extract)
2 tablespoons plain flour
½ teaspoon coarse salt
⅓ cup (50 grams) raisins
2⅛ ounces (60 grams) unsalted
  butter, softened to room
  temperature
1 to 2 tablespoons icing sugar, as
  needed

kalyta

honey-glazed poppy-seed loaf   *Калита*

This traditional bread has long been prepared in Ukraine for the feast of Andrew the Apostle, which is celebrated on December 13. In the past on this day, despite the fast, young people were allowed to hold parties and enjoy themselves. The girls would make a delicious bread shaped like a circle and hang it in the middle of the house, and the boys would have to grab it with their mouths and bite off a piece.

Kalyta is quite dense and looks like gingerbread. Although the holiday isn't widely celebrated today, some homemakers still make kalyta and hang it in the house.

1 cup (120 grams) poppy seeds
½ cup (100 grams) sugar
4 cups (540 grams) plain flour
1 teaspoon baking powder
Pinch of coarse salt
1 cup (250 millilitres) warm water
3 tablespoons sunflower oil
3 tablespoons chopped walnuts
3 tablespoons dried cranberries or raisins
2 tablespoons honey

1. In a medium bowl, stir together the poppy seeds and sugar.

2. Add the flour to a large mixing bowl and whisk in the baking powder and salt. Slowly drizzle in the water and mix everything thoroughly until a shaggy dough forms. Stir in the oil and most of the poppy-seed mixture (leave about 2 tablespoons to decorate the kalyta with). Stir in the walnuts and cranberries, also saving a little to decorate the bread with.

3. Using your hands (I suggest greasing them with a little oil to keep the dough from sticking too much), knead the dough until it becomes smooth and elastic. Shape it into a ball and place it in a greased bowl. Cover the bowl with a kitchen towel and let rest for about 20 minutes.

4. While the dough is resting, preheat the oven to 190°C/375°F/Gas 5 and line a large baking sheet with baking paper.

5. Remove the dough from the bowl and, using your hands, carefully make a hole in the centre of the ball. Pull at the dough slightly to stretch it out a little. Place the dough on the lined baking sheet and shape it into a circle. Sprinkle the saved poppy seeds, walnuts, and cranberries on top of the kalyta and press them down into the dough a little. Bake in the preheated oven for 30 minutes. Once it is baked through and has a golden crust, drizzle some honey over the loaf.

apple cookies with hamula mousse

Печиво з яблуками та гамулою

The earliest mention of hamula in print can be found in Zinovia Klinovetska's 1913 cookbook, but most likely hamula was prepared earlier than that. According to various sources, in the old days, the preparation of this dessert began in the fall. Ukrainians realized that the bruised apples they were keeping in the cellar couldn't be stored for long, so they baked them, puréed them, added flour, honey, and oats, then slowly baked them again at a low temperature in the oven. Inspired by this dessert, I decided to cook a light apple mousse and serve it with simple apple cookies. Well, it's a nice way to pay homage to traditions.

1. Preheat the oven to 200°C/400°F/Gas 6. Arrange the apple halves cut-side down on a baking sheet lined with baking paper or aluminum foil and bake for approximately 40 minutes or until soft.

2. Once the apples have cooled a little, remove the skins and purée the apples using a blender or food processor. The purée will be used for both the cookie dough and the mousse. You should have about a cup (250 millilitres) of purée.

3. To make the cookie dough, whisk together both flours, the sugar, and a pinch of salt in a medium mixing bowl. Stir in the cubed butter and rub it into the flour mixture with your hands until the texture resembles wet sand and no large lumps of butter remain. Whisk in the egg and about ½ cup (120 millilitres) of the puréed apple and knead until a dense dough forms. Cover the dough with plastic wrap and leave it in the fridge for 20 to 30 minutes.

4. Place the dough between two sheets of baking paper and roll it out to a thickness of ¼ inch (5 millimetres). Cut out cookie shapes using a glass or a cookie cutter and arrange them on a baking-paper-lined baking sheet.

5. Bake in the preheated oven for 7 to 10 minutes until golden. Cool.

6. Meanwhile, make the apple mousse: in a heatproof bowl, whisk together the remaining apple purée, the egg yolks, the milk, and the sugar. Place the bowl over a saucepan of simmering water and, stirring continuously, cook for about 10 minutes or until the mixture thickens enough to coat the back of a spoon. Remove from the heat and let cool completely before serving along with the cookies.

for the cookie dough

3 large tart apples, such as Granny Smith, halved and cored
¾ cup (100 grams) plain flour
½ cup plus 1 tablespoon (75 grams) oat flour
2 tablespoons granulated sugar
Coarse salt
2⅛ ounces (60 grams) unsalted butter, cubed
1 large egg

for the hamula mousse

3 large egg yolks
½ cup (120 millilitres) milk
2 tablespoons granulated sugar

baked apples
with soft cheese

Запечені яблука з сиром

makes 4
baked apples

start to finish:
1 hour

If you're not big on candy or cakes but still occasionally crave something sweet, try these baked apples stuffed with soft cheese and honey. This recipe is, in my opinion, a kind of modern interpretation of hamula (see the recipe for Apple Cookies with Hamula Mousse, page 230). They're delicious, packed with nutrients, and made with easy-to-find ingredients. And they're also a hit
with kids!

4 large tart apples, such as
   Granny Smith
Unsalted butter
1 cup (225 grams) soft cheese
Handful of chopped walnuts
Handful of raisins
3 tablespoons honey

1. Preheat the oven to 190°C/375°F/Gas 5. Cut apple tops and bottoms off and carefully core them with a spoon, being careful not to break the apples. Grease a medium baking dish with about a teaspoon of butter and arrange the cored apples in it. Set aside.

2. Make the filling: Combine the soft cheese, chopped nuts, raisins, and honey in a small bowl. Spoon even portions of the filling into each apple.

3. Place the filled apples in the preheated oven and bake for 35 to 40 minutes or until soft. The baking time will vary depending on the type and size of the apples.

simpler kyiv candied fruit

Швидкий рецепт київського сухого варення

serves 4 to 6

start to finish:
*2 hours
15 minutes*

Kyiv has long been known for its dry jam—candied fruit, usually served with coffee or tea. According to the nineteenth-century Ukrainian ethnographer and historian Mykola Zakrevskyi, Kyiv candied fruit was served in the fourteenth century at formal banquets of the Lithuanian prince. It's challenging to verify information from so long ago, but we do know that in the nineteenth century, the Balabukh family, Kyiv entrepreneurs residing in Podil (a renowned trading area of the Ukrainian capital), began making candied fruits and selling them at their store on Khreshchatyk Street.

The recipe for Kyiv candied fruit can be found in Zinovia Klinovetska's 1913 cookbook. It can be made from any fruit—apples, pears, strawberries, and even cherries. The key to its preparation is drying the boiled fruits completely and coating them with sugar so they can be stored for several months.

Here I simplify the original recipe a bit by skipping the initial process of making a thick fruit jam; instead, I dry the fruit in the oven with sugar right away. It's delicious. You can store this dry jam in a cool place for up to a month.

2 pounds (1 kilogram) firm sweet apples
1¼ cups (250 grams) granulated sugar, plus another 1¼ cups (250 grams) to toss the dried apples in
1 teaspoon ground cinnamon
1 teaspoon citric acid powder

1. Wash the apples well, pat them dry, and core them. Cut the apples into thick slices and set them aside. Preheat the oven to 190°C/375°F/Gas 5.

2. In a large mixing bowl, whisk together the sugar, cinnamon, and citric acid powder. Toss the apple slices in the mixture and lay them out on a parchment-lined baking sheet. Bake in the preheated oven for 30 minutes, remove the apples, and let them cool completely. Let the oven cool to 140°C/275°F/Gas 1. Arrange the apples on another parchment-lined baking sheet and bake them for 1 to 2 hours or until they have dried sufficiently. Turn them over halfway through.

3. Remove the apples from the oven, toss them with the remaining sugar, and serve.

cherry and poppy-seed varenyky

serves 4 | start to finish: *40 minutes*

pictured on pages 238–239

Вареники з вишнями та маком

Varenyky are beloved traditional Ukrainian dumplings and so widely known that I wondered if writing about them was unnecessary. But in the end I couldn't keep myself from sharing my recipe for cherry varenyky, an iconic dessert that you're bound to come across in any Ukrainian restaurant. See my recipe for a savoury version, Varenyky with Potato and Cabbage Fillings, on page 186.

In this recipe you'll also find a small tip to help you keep the dumplings juicy but prevent the cherry juice from spilling all over the place as soon as you take a bite.

¾ pound (350 grams) fresh or frozen cherries, pitted
2½ cups (340 grams) plain flour, plus extra for dusting
½ cup plus 2 tablespoons (150 millilitres) water
3 tablespoons sunflower oil (or other neutral oil), plus extra to grease your hands
Large pinch of coarse salt
2 tablespoons granulated sugar
1 tablespoon (12 grams) semolina flour or cornflour
1 teaspoon poppy seeds
Butter
Honey and soured cream (optional, for serving)

1. If using frozen cherries, take them out of the freezer and let them thaw until no longer frozen but still firm.

2. Meanwhile, in a large bowl, combine the flour, water, 3 tablespoons oil, and salt. Mix with your hands until a shaggy dough forms. Knead the dough until elastic but not too smooth, about 5 minutes, oiling your hands to keep it from sticking too much. Form the dough into a ball and let it rest for 10 to 15 minutes. This will help the gluten relax and keep the varenyky from becoming too chewy.

3. In a small bowl, toss the cherries with the sugar and semolina or cornflour. This step ensures the cherry filling will thicken while remaining juicy. Add the poppy seeds and mix everything to combine.

4. Roll the dough out on a lightly floured surface until it is just under ⅛ inch (3 millimetres) thick. Using either a glass or a 3-inch (7.5-centimetre) cookie cutter, cut out round shapes. Make the shapes as close together as possible, and keep the scraps. Once you have used up all the dough, gather the leftover scraps, roll them into a ball, and repeat the process.

5. Place about three cherries in the centre of each circle of dough, fold the dough in half, and pinch the edges together to seal, making a half-moon shape. Crimp the edges with your fingers or the tines of a fork. Place the prepared varenyky on a floured baking sheet to prevent sticking.

6. Fill a large, heavy-based pot with water and bring it to a boil over medium heat.

7. Once the water in the saucepan has come to a rolling boil, gently drop the varenyky into the saucepan and cook them for 5 to 7 minutes or until they float to the surface and the dough is soft and tender. Fish them out using a spider or a large slotted spoon and place them in a large bowl. Toss with a little butter to keep the varenyky from sticking together.

8. Serve hot with a little honey on top and soured cream on the side (optional).

Drinks

rye bread kvas

Хлібний квас

makes about
2 quarts
(2 litres)

start to finish:
3 to 7 days
(20 minutes
active time)

1 pound (450 grams) dark rye
  bread
10 cups (2.5 litres) water
¼ cup (50 grams) granulated
  sugar
¼ teaspoon easy-bake/fast-action
yeast
Handful of raisins

Kvas, or syrivets, as it was once called, is one of the most well-known Ukrainian beverages; it dates back to the times of Kyivan Rus. In the ancient recipe for making bread kvas, toasted rye or oat grains were used along with toasted rye breadcrumbs. Later, it was made by adding yeast. Toasted rye bread was soaked in boiling water, and after it cooled down, a starter or yeast was added. When the kvas was sufficiently fermented, it was strained. The modern method is not much different from this. However, I suggest adding raisins, as they give the drink a pleasant fruity note.

You can make kvas from pumpernickel or any other type of rye bread. Since the process involves fermentation and depends on various environmental factors, you need to pay attention to prevent overfermentation. I recommend draining some of the kvas on the third day of preparation. When you see enough bubbles in it and it doesn't taste too bland, you can strain it, bottle it, and put it in the fridge.

1. Roughly cube the dark rye bread and toast it in a dry frying pan over medium heat until fragrant and toasty.

2. In a mixing bowl, combine 1 cup (250 millilitres) water with the sugar and yeast. Whisk until the sugar has fully dissolved.

3. Transfer the toasted rye bread into a half-gallon (2-litre) glass jar with a screw-on lid. Add the sugar and yeast mixture and the raisins. Add enough water to almost fill the jar and stir a little with a long spoon or a chopstick to combine. Cover with the lid (but do not screw it on tightly) and let the mixture rest in a dark place at room temperature for 3 to 7 days or until lightly carbonated. It should be fizzy and have a sweet, slightly nutty aroma reminiscent of rye bread.

4. Filter the kvas through a sieve lined with muslin, transfer the liquid to an airtight container, and store in the fridge. Kvas can be kept in the fridge for up to ten days.

beetroot kvas

makes about 8¾ cups (2 litres)	start to finish: *3 to 4 days* *(20 minutes* *active time)*

Буряковий квас

1 pound (450 grams) beetroots
10 cups (2.5 litres) water
1 cup (200 grams) sugar

Beetroot kvas is a traditional Ukrainian drink that appears in our oldest culinary manuscripts. Historically, kvas wasn't just a refreshing beverage; it was added to meat stews and to borsch and used as a base for various cold soups. The question of how much sugar should be added is hotly debated. I'll tell you one thing: It depends on how sweet you like your drinks and how much time you've got. If you reduce the amount of sugar, the fermentation time increases by a week or two. This particular recipe I'm sharing calls for quite a lot of sugar, so it ferments very quickly.

In ancient recipes, beetroot kvas was prepared without sugar. The beetroots were soaked in cold water, and sometimes a few slices of rye bread were added. Without sugar, it took several weeks to make kvas.

1. Wash the beetroots, peel them, finely dice them, and transfer them to a 12 cup (3-litre) glass jar with a screw-on lid. They should take up two-thirds of the jar.

2. Bring the water to a boil and let it cool to room temperature.

3. Add the sugar to the jar with the beetroots. Once the water has cooled, add enough water to the jar to fully submerge the beetroots. The beetroots should be covered by 1 to 2 inches (3 to 5 centimetres) of water.

4. Cover the jar with a large piece of muslin folded in four layers and let it rest in a warm, draft-free space for three or four days. When bubbles begin to appear on the surface, that means the fermentation process is underway.

5. After three or four days, store the kvas in the fridge. Serve cool.

uzvar

makes 12 cups
(3 litres)

start to finish:
30 minutes

traditional dried-fruit drink   *Узвар*

Uzvar is another iconic Ukrainian drink. In the old days, uzvar referred not only to a decoction made from dried fruit but also one made from fresh fruit, depending on the season. Today, the term *kompot* is more commonly used for a beverage made from fresh fruit (see the recipe for Cherry Kompot, page 248).

Uzvar was prepared for everyday consumption and for holidays, especially during Christmas. It was also used as a remedy for vitamin deficiency in spring. Cooks added it to Kutya (page 212) to enhance its flavour, and the boiled fruits were not discarded; they were mashed and used in baking or as a filling for varenyky.

Traditionally, sugar was not added to uzvar, but I like to enhance the flavour a bit with honey and smoked paprika.

¾ pound (350 grams) dried or smoked pears, prunes, apricots, and apples
12 cups (3 litres) cold water
scant 2/3 cup (150 millilitres) honey
3 whole cloves
1½ teaspoons smoked paprika

1. Wash the dried fruit well under cold running water and add to a large saucepan. Cover with cold water and bring to a boil over medium heat. Reduce the heat, cover, and let simmer for about 30 minutes or until fragrant and golden brown.

2. Take off the heat and stir in the honey, cloves, and smoked paprika.

3. If needed, adjust the sweetness by adding a little more honey just before serving.

cherry kompot

makes 10 cups
(2.5 litres)

start to finish:
20 minutes

Компот

Kompots—sweet beverages made with berries and fruit—are hugely popular in Ukraine, especially in the summer. The best thing about this beverage is that you can make it using any kind of fruit that's available and adjust the amount of sugar according to the sweetness of the fruit and your own preferences. Some excellent combinations include strawberries with mint, cherries with currants, and apples with pears. Unlike a decoction, kompot, which is made from fresh berries and fruits, does not have a smoky aftertaste.

The main thing to keep in mind is that you don't need to stew the fruit for a long time—just bring the water to a boil and let the fruit cook for a few minutes.

1 pound (450 grams) frozen
  cherries, pitted
1 cup (200 grams) sugar (more or
  less, to your preference)
10 cups (2.5 litres) water
10 to 12 sprigs elderberry flowers,
  to taste
1 cinnamon stick

1. Combine the cherries, sugar, and water in a large saucepan. Add the elderberry flower and the cinnamon stick. Bring the mixture to a boil over medium heat, reduce the heat, and let the mixture simmer for a few minutes or until the sugar dissolves completely.

2. Remove the saucepan from the heat, discard the elderberry flower sprigs and the cinnamon, and let the drink cool completely before serving. It will keep in the fridge for about a week.

kysil

starchy berry drink   *Кисіль*

Kysil—a starchy, viscous drink made from berries or other fruit and thickened with cornflour—isn't as popular as Cherry Kompot (page 248), but it dates back to the time of the Kyivan Rus. In that ancient era, the word *kysil* referred to a sour infusion made from ground roasted oats. It was served alongside savoury dishes and sometimes flavoured with berries. Later on, people started making kysil with starch, and berries became an integral part of this drink.

The process is similar to making kompot, but the beverage is thickened with cornflour or potato starch, which gives it a unique texture. It might take a little getting used to, but you should definitely try this beverage at least once!

12 cups (3 litres) water
½ cup plus 2 tablespoons
   (110 grams) granulated sugar
14 ounces (400 grams) assorted
   berries, fresh or frozen and
   thawed
5 tablespoons cornflour

1. Bring the water to a boil in a large saucepan over medium heat and whisk in the sugar. Wait for it to completely dissolve, then add the berries of your choosing. Reduce the heat to low and simmer the mixture for about 10 minutes or until it becomes fragrant and takes on a deep berry colour.

2. Dissolve the cornflour in ½ cup (120 millilitres) cold water and gradually drizzle it into the simmering berry-infused water, whisking constantly to keep it from becoming lumpy.

3. Simmer the kysil for a few more minutes or until it thickens a little. It will thicken even more once it cools, so there is no need to cook it for long. Remove the kysil from the heat and let cool at room temperature.

4. If you like, filter out the berries before serving.

lemonade with honey and mint

Лимонад з медом та м'ятою

The culture of making lemonade is relatively new in Ukraine, because we've historically drunk kvas, kompot, and kysil in the summer. But many Ukrainians have come to enjoy the pleasant citrus acidity so much that this refreshing drink is now a national favourite, so I decided to share a special recipe for my signature honey lemonade.

1 whole lemon, peeled
1 whole orange, peeled
½ cup (120 millilitres) honey
10 cups (2.5 litres) water
5 sprigs mint

1. Cut the lemon and orange into halves. Chop half the fruit into large chunks and blitz them in a blender, adding a little water if necessary. Put the fruit purée in a medium saucepan, add the honey and 2 cups (500 millilitres) water, and bring to a boil over medium heat. Reduce the heat, simmer the mixture for about 5 minutes, and let cool before straining the fruit-infused syrup through a sieve.

2. In a large jar, combine the fruit syrup with the remaining 2 quarts (2 litres) water. Slice the remaining fruit and add it to the lemonade along with the mint. Serve the lemonade over ice, adjusting the taste with a little more honey if desired.

sour cherry nalyvka

infused liqueur

Наливка з вишень

makes
about 1 pint
(500 millilitres)

start to finish:
3 to 4 weeks
(20 minutes
active time)

If I had to bet on what the most popular hard drink in Ukraine is, I'd choose nalyvka—a liqueur infused with berries, fruit, or even vegetables. The most famous and delicious of them all is cherry liqueur. By the way, you don't need to wait for cherry season, because you can make this using frozen cherries and it'll taste just as good.

2 pounds (900 grams) fresh or thawed frozen sour cherries, pitted
1½ cups (300 grams) granulated sugar
1 to 2 sticks cinnamon
2½ cups (570 millilitres) cognac or brandy

1. Add the cherries and any juice from them to a 4-cup-size (1-litre) glass jar.

2. Add the sugar to the cherries and place the cinnamon sticks on top. Add the cognac or brandy. Seal and shake the jar. Keep it in the fridge for three or four weeks, shaking the jar daily to make sure the cherries release all their juices and the sugar dissolves.

3. The liqueur will be ready in three to four weeks; just remember to give it a good shake every day or two. Once it is ready, strain out the cherries. The liqueur will keep in the fridge for up to a year.

blackcurrant nalyvka

infused liqueur　　　　　　　　　　　*Наливка зі смородини*

makes about
4 cups (1 litre)　|　start to finish:
*2 weeks or more
(20 minutes
active time)*

This is another popular version of berry-infused liqueur like Sour
Cherry Nalyvka (page 255). This time it's made with blackcurrants, but
you could use raspberries, blackberries, or strawberries. Of course, this
drink tastes best when prepared with fresh berries just picked off the
branch and still warm from the summer sun. But it'll be delicious even
if you make it using frozen store-bought berries.

Although fennel seeds are not a traditional ingredient in Ukrainian
infusions, I add them to give a refreshing flavour to the drink.

2 cups (400 grams) granulated
　sugar
2 pounds (1 kilogram) fresh
　or frozen and thawed
　blackcurrants
½ teaspoon fennel seeds
2¼ cups (525 millilitres) vodka

1. Dissolve the sugar in about 1 cup (250 millilitres) water and bring to a
   boil over low heat. Let the mixture simmer until it thickens into a light
   syrup. Remove it from the heat.

2. In a large glass jar, muddle the blackcurrants with the fennel seeds and
   pour the simple syrup over the berries. Add the vodka, seal the jar with
   a lid, and shake it well.

3. Place the jar in the fridge for at least two weeks—the flavour will get
   more intense over time, so don't rush it.

khrinovuha

horseradish-infused vodka   *Хріновуха*

makes about 4 cups (1 litre)	start to finish: *1 month (10 minutes active time)*

One 2- to 3-inch (100-gram) piece fresh horseradish, unpeeled
One 750-millilitre bottle vodka

In addition to sweet berry liqueurs, Ukrainians have historically enjoyed bitter, strong tinctures infused with herbs or roots. One popular drink that can be found in every Ukrainian bar and restaurant is a horseradish-infused vodka called khrinovuha. If you're worried about this drink being too hot or pungent, don't be—during the infusion process, the intense taste of horseradish disappears and leaves a pleasantly sweet aftertaste.

1. Using a box grater or a Microplane, finely grate the fresh unpeeled horseradish. Transfer it to a 4-cup-size (1-litre) glass jar that has a lid.

2. Pour the vodka into the jar with the horseradish. Put the lid on the jar and shake it well. Place it in the fridge.

3. Let the vodka steep for at least three days and up to one month. Taste it every once in a while; when the horseradish flavour is as strong as you like, strain the vodka into a clean container.

drinks

259

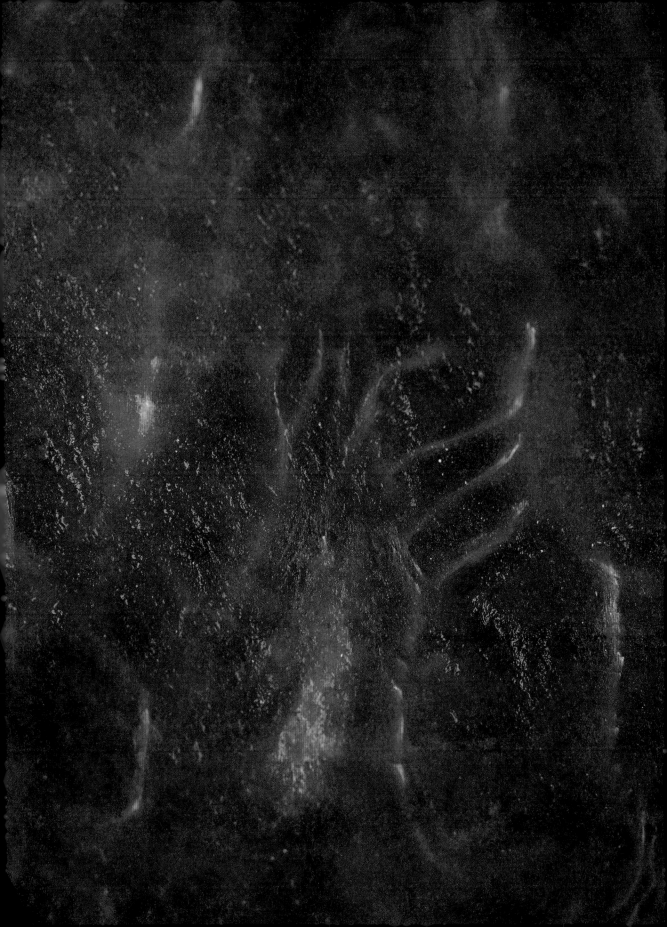

index

about the author

YEVHEN KLOPOTENKO is a Ukrainian chef, restaurateur, cookbook author, and social activist. His popular cooking website Klopotenko.com promotes authentic Ukrainian cuisine across the country and the world. He is renowned for changing school meals so that children could become educated about Ukrainian culinary traditions and heritage. In 2015 he won season 5 of *MasterChef Ukraine*. In 2016 he graduated from Le Cordon Bleu cooking school in Paris. In 2019, Klopotenko opened 100 Years Back to the Future, a restaurant in Kyiv that combines Ukrainian culinary heritage with modern techniques. In 2021 he was named one of the 50 Next, a list of people shaping the future of gastronomy. In 2022, he opened Inshi Bistro in Lviv, which was followed by the Inshi bar in 2023. Also in 2023, he opened the restaurant Poltava in Kyiv. He is currently devoting efforts to humanitarian aid in Ukraine. Born in Kyiv, he studied international relations at the Kyiv University of Economics and Law and has worked in the United States, the United Kingdom, and Europe.